CASH FLOW CURE

Stop Worrying and Start Loving Your Business Again

Christopher O'Neal, CPA, MBA

ISBN: 9798345132968

DEDICATION

To my amazing parents, whose unwavering support and belief in me have been a constant, even when I didn't make it easy. To my incredible wife, who doubles as my business partner – because clearly, I don't get enough of her at home. And to my wonderful kids, who inspire me to be a better person (and who also provide excellent material for awkward family stories).

FOREWARD

It's Time to Make Your Numbers Work for You

"If you're not having fun, you're doing something wrong."

– Groucho Marx

If the thought of financial statements, cash flow forecasts, or business structures makes you want to curl up under a blanket with Netflix and a snack, you're not alone. For most business owners, **"finance" feels like a necessary evil**—something you deal with begrudgingly, usually right before tax season. But here's the thing: **Mastering your business's finances doesn't have to be painful.** In fact, it can be downright empowering.

Whether you're running an **e-commerce shop, managing an HOA, or building your dream crypto business from scratch,** understanding your numbers is the key to success. And no—you don't have to be a financial wizard to figure it out. This book, "Cash Flow Cure: Simple Strategies," will show you how to master the essentials in a way that's practical, approachable, and yes, even fun.

What You Can Expect from This Book

Throughout the nine chapters, you'll learn how to **ditch the confusion** around your finances and take control of the numbers that drive your business. Here's a taste of what's inside:

- **Financial Clarity** is your starting point. You'll learn how to read key reports like your profit & loss statement (without your eyes glazing over) and figure out exactly where your business stands. **It's like GPS for your business—if you know where you are, you'll know where to go next.**
- **Profitability** is the art of turning revenue into something that actually sticks around. You'll uncover the difference between making sales and making money—and how companies like **Tesla** figured this out the hard way.

- **Cash Flow Management** keeps the lights on. You'll learn how Netflix survived its early cash crunch, and why running out of cash—even when you're profitable—can still sink a business.
- **Financial Planning** will help you set goals you can actually hit. You'll discover how tools like **AI-powered forecasts** (hello, ChatGPT!) are making it easier than ever to plan for the future, without giving you a headache.
- **Tools and Tech** make managing your money simpler. From accounting software to **crypto wallets** and automated invoicing, you'll see how smart tools can help you save time and stay organized.
- **Taxes and Regulations** aren't just a chore—they're a game you can win if you play it right. Whether you're navigating **e-commerce tax laws** or figuring out how to report **crypto payments**, we've got you covered.
- **AI and Automation** are here to make your life easier—but only if you use them wisely. This book will show you how to **balance automation with a personal touch,** so you don't lose that human connection with customers.
- **Business Formation** isn't just about choosing a name—it's a financial strategy. You'll learn when to level up from LLC to S Corp (and how to save big on taxes), with a real-world example of a freelancer who made the switch at the perfect time.
- And finally, **The People Factor** teaches you how to get the most out of your team. Engaged employees aren't just happy—they're productive and profitable, too. We'll explore how companies like Zappos and Netflix use employee engagement to boost profits, and how you can do the same.

This Isn't Just a Finance Book—It's Your New Business Playbook

Every chapter in this book builds on the last, giving you a **complete roadmap to mastering your business finances.** But don't worry—**there's no jargon, no confusing math, and no dull lectures.** Instead, you'll get real-world examples, helpful tips, and practical advice you can use immediately.

Think of this book as a **friendly guide**—the kind of advice you'd get from a savvy business mentor over coffee (or something stronger). It's not about turning you into an accountant—it's about **giving you the tools and confidence to make smart financial decisions.** And if you ever feel stuck, remember: The Nealson Group is here to help. We're only a phone call away.

Your Journey to Financial Freedom Starts Here

By the end of this book, you'll be equipped to:

- Track your financial health with clarity.
- Increase your profits without chasing pointless revenue.
- Manage your cash flow so you're never caught off guard.
- Use tools and technology to streamline your operations.
- Navigate taxes and compliance with confidence.
- Engage your employees to boost productivity and profitability.
- Choose the right business structure to save money and reduce headaches.

This book is about **taking control**—of your finances, your business, and your future. It's not about perfection. It's about **progress**. And every small step you take in understanding your finances will bring you closer to the financial freedom you've been working toward.

So, grab a cup of coffee (or your favorite beverage) and dive in. **Let's get your business—and your finances—on the path to success.**

YOU'VE GOT THIS.

And If You Need a Little Extra Help...

We get it—sometimes, knowing where to start is half the battle. That's where **The Nealson Group** comes in. Whether you need help with **cash flow forecasting, business formation, tax planning, or anything in between**, we're here to help you turn your goals into reality.

So as you read through these chapters and start putting things into action, **know that you're not alone.** If you ever feel stuck or need personalized guidance, **give us a call at 561.299.1020 or send us an email at** consultations@nealsongroup.com and request a callback.

Let's make this the year you finally take control of your business finances—and unlock the freedom you've been working toward.

CONTENTS

ACKNOWLEDGMENTS

A huge shout-out to everyone who's ever launched a business, pitched an idea, or faced a spreadsheet with a mixture of terror and determination. Keep hustling, keep innovating, and keep laughing (especially when things go hilariously wrong – because they will). You are the reason I wrote this book. May it provide some useful insights, a few good laughs, and maybe even a tiny bit of comfort when you inevitably spill coffee on your business plan.

Chapter 1: Financial Clarity – Seeing Through the Fog

"The secret of getting ahead is getting started." – Mark Twain

This chapter keeps it light, funny, and informative, with practical advice that non-financial peeps can actually use. Enjoy your journey.

Introduction: Why Clarity Is the New Cool

Let's face it—most business owners didn't start their journey dreaming about spreadsheets or profit-and-loss statements. You probably had a vision, right? Maybe you imagined launching the next big e-commerce brand, creating a close-knit community oasis through your HOA, or creating the next groundbreaking cryptocurrency venture. Your dream probably didn't involve late nights wrestling with accounting software or puzzling over balance sheets.

But here's the truth: Without financial clarity, running a business is like driving in the fog with no headlights. You might be moving, but you have no idea if you're heading toward success—or straight into a ditch. The goal of this chapter? To help you wipe that windshield clean so you can see where you're going. Financial clarity might sound complex, but really, it's just about understanding where your business stands—and what you need to do next.

1. The Three Magic Numbers: Balance Sheet, Profit & Loss, and Cash Flow

Imagine these three as your business's best friends. Each has a unique personality and tells you something vital. Ignore them, and you'll have a tough time down the road.

- **The Balance Sheet**: *Why it matters:* Knowing your *'what I own vs. what I owe'* snapshot gives you the confidence to make investment decisions, identify debt issues early, and know exactly where your money is tied up.

- Assets on one side, liabilities on the other. If your assets aren't covering your liabilities, well... let's just say that's like owning a car worth less than the loan on it—tricky, right?

- To break it down further, think of your assets as everything your business owns that has value. This could include the cash you have on hand, the equipment you use to run your operations, any property you own, and even the money that customers owe you (accounts receivable).

- On the flip side, liabilities represent everything your business owes to others. This could include loans you've taken out, credit card balances, unpaid bills to suppliers, or any other outstanding debts. A healthy balance sheet typically shows that your assets outweigh your liabilities, giving you a solid financial foundation. If your liabilities consistently exceed your assets, it could be a red flag that you're relying too heavily on debt and might need to adjust your spending or find ways to generate more income.

Pro Tip: Review it at least once a quarter to ensure you're not slowly sliding underwater.

- **Profit and Loss (P&L) Statement**: *Why it matters:* Tracking your P&L helps you spot patterns in spending or income, allowing you to act before things spiral.

- This one tells the story of your business over time. Are you making more than you're spending? If not, no amount of sales will save you. It's like trying to lose weight—you can't just eat salads twice a week and hope for miracles if you're also hitting the drive-thru daily.

- The P&L statement provides a clear picture of your revenue and expenses over a specific period, such as a month, quarter, or year. Think of it as a detailed breakdown of your business's financial performance. It shows you where your money is coming from (sales, services, etc.) and where it's going (rent, salaries, marketing costs, etc.). By analyzing your P&L statement regularly, you can identify trends in your revenue and expenses, spot potential areas for cost savings, and make informed decisions about pricing, inventory, and overall business strategy.

Pro Tip: Review this monthly to avoid surprises like a dip in profits. For example, take a look at Spotify's financial journey—they have high recurring costs, so they monitor P&Ls closely to keep subscriber numbers high and offset expenses.

- **Cash Flow Statement**: *Why it matters:* Cash flow keeps your business alive. Even a profitable business can crash without cash on hand to pay bills.

- Cash flow is the one friend who tells you the brutal truth. It doesn't care if you're making a million dollars in sales—if there's no cash in your account, it's lights out. That's why profitable businesses still go belly-up.

- Think of your cash flow statement as a river flowing through your business. Money comes in from sales, loans, or investments (that's the water flowing into the river). Money goes out to pay for expenses like rent, supplies, and salaries (that's the water flowing out). The cash flow statement tracks this constant ebb and flow, showing you where your cash is coming from and where it's going.

- Now, imagine a dam suddenly blocking the river. Even if there's plenty of water further upstream (like future sales), the water below the dam (your available cash) might dry up. That's why even profitable businesses can fail – they might have lots of promised income, but not enough cash on hand to cover immediate expenses. The cash flow statement helps you identify those potential "dams" and find ways to keep the river flowing smoothly.

- To really understand where your cash is going, the cash flow statement is divided into three main sections:
  - **Operating Activities:** This is like your business's daily routine. It includes all the cash coming in from your core business operations (like customers paying for your products or services) and the cash going out to cover everyday expenses (like paying your employees, rent, or utility bills). Think of it as tracking the money you earn from doing what you do best and the money you spend to keep the lights on.

- **Investing Activities:** This section focuses on bigger-picture stuff, like buying or selling long-term assets. For example, if you purchase a new piece of equipment for your business, that would show up here. Or, if you sell an old delivery van, that would also be recorded in this section. It's all about tracking the cash flow related to investments that help your business grow and operate.
- **Financing Activities:** This section deals with how you get the money to fund your business. It includes things like taking out loans, receiving investments, or paying dividends to shareholders. Think of it as tracking the cash flow related to how your business is financed – where the money comes from to get started and keep growing.

- Imagine your business is a house. Operating activities are like paying the monthly bills to keep the house running. Investing activities are like making renovations or buying new furniture. Financing activities are like getting a mortgage to buy the house in the first place.

- If you own a coffee shop, operating activities would include the cash from selling coffee and pastries and the cash used to pay your baristas and buy coffee beans. Investing activities might involve buying a new espresso machine. Financing activities could include getting a loan to open a second location.

- Let's say you land a big client who promises to pay $50,000 in 60 days. That's great for your P&L, but your cash flow statement will show that you won't actually have that cash for two months. In the meantime, you need to make sure you have enough cash to cover your expenses until that payment arrives.

- Just like checking the weather forecast helps you prepare for rain, your cash flow statement helps you anticipate potential cash shortages and take steps to avoid them. Maybe you need to negotiate better payment terms with clients, secure a line of credit, or temporarily reduce expenses.

> **Pro Tip**: Forecasting cash flow is like checking the weather before heading out. It won't prevent storms, but at least you can carry an umbrella.

2. KPIs: The Secret Sauce for Tracking Clarity

KPIs—Key Performance Indicators—are like your business's report card, minus the nerve-wracking parent-teacher conference. You don't need dozens of them to stay on top of your finances; just a few key ones will do the trick.

Here are the most impactful KPIs to track:

Current Ratio:

> *What it is:* The Current Ratio measures your business's liquidity by comparing assets to liabilities.
> *Why it matters:* A high Current Ratio shows you're in a solid position to meet short-term obligations. If your ratio is low (below 1.0), it might signal liquidity issues, indicating that your business could struggle to cover its debts.
> *Formula:* Current Assets ÷ Current Liabilities

- A quick look at liquidity. If you've got $2 in assets for every $1 in liabilities, you're in a solid position.
- Below 1.0? It may signal liquidity issues.

Gross Profit Margin:

> *What it is:* This metric calculates how much of each dollar earned is left after covering the Cost of Goods Sold (COGS).

Why it matters: Gross Profit Margin shows whether your core business is profitable before other expenses, like rent and salaries, kick in. A margin above 20% is generally considered healthy, while a lower margin might mean it's time to reassess your costs or pricing strategy.
Formula: (Revenue - COGS) ÷ Revenue × 100

- This shows how much of each dollar is left after covering essentials. Aim for more than just "barely staying afloat." Consider the journey of small, rapidly growing e-commerce brands like Glossier—they closely monitor this margin to sustain growth.
- Above 20% is often healthy; below 10% could mean you need to evaluate costs.

Days Sales Outstanding (DSO):

What it is: DSO tracks the average time it takes for you to get paid after a sale.
Why it matters: The longer it takes to collect payments, the more cash flow is affected. Aim for fewer than 45 days to keep cash flowing smoothly. If your DSO is high, it may be worth reviewing payment terms or incentivizing quicker payments.
Formula: (Accounts Receivable ÷ Total Credit Sales) × Number of Days

- How long it takes to get paid. If it takes longer than a new Taylor Swift album to drop, you've got a problem.
- Aim for fewer than 45 days; anything longer might slow cash flow.

Burn Rate:

What it is: Burn Rate calculates how quickly your business is spending its cash reserves.
Why it matters: This metric is critical for businesses with variable

revenue. If your monthly Burn Rate exceeds 20% of cash reserves, it could be a warning sign that you need to reduce costs or secure additional funding.
Formula: Cash Spent Per Month

- Especially important for startups, burn rate is the speed at which you're using cash reserves. Think of Uber in its early days; its burn rate was massive, so they monitored this obsessively to ensure they had enough cash until they hit profitability.
- Burn Rate Benchmarks to Watch:

Monthly:

- o **Under 10% of cash reserves per month:** This is typically a safe zone, allowing the business to sustain operations for an extended period if revenue stalls or drops.
- o **10-20% of cash reserves per month:** This is manageable but indicates a need for close monitoring. If revenue drops unexpectedly, you may need to take cost-cutting measures.
- o **Over 20% of cash reserves per month:** This could be a red flag. At this rate, the business will deplete its cash reserves quickly, potentially leading to financial stress unless it can secure additional funding or increase revenue rapidly.

- **Cash Lifeline:** This is the time the business has before cash reserves are exhausted at the current burn rate.
  - o **12+ months:** Generally healthy. This amount of runway offers flexibility and allows for strategic investments without immediate pressure to turn profits.
  - o **6-12 months:** This is still decent but indicates that the business should start planning for either increased revenue or reduced expenses if profitability isn't in sight.

- o **Under 6 months**: This is a critical warning sign, suggesting that the business either needs a cash infusion or a serious reduction in spending to survive.

- **Trends in Burn Rate**:
  - o **Rising Burn Rate**: If your burn rate is increasing month-over-month, look for specific expenses that might be escalating and assess whether they're necessary. For example, is the increase due to growing overhead costs, marketing expenses, or payroll? Rising burn rates without a correlating increase in revenue or new funding can quickly become unsustainable.
  - o **Steady or Declining Burn Rate**: If your burn rate is stable or declining, that's a good sign. It means you're managing expenses effectively, especially if revenue is growing or holding steady.

- Beyond the basics, there are a few other KPIs that can provide valuable insights into your business's performance. **Net Profit Margin** goes beyond gross profit margin to show how much profit you keep for every dollar earned after *all* expenses are paid, including taxes and interest. **Customer Acquisition Cost (CAC)** helps you understand how much it costs to acquire a new customer, which is crucial for evaluating the effectiveness of your marketing campaigns. And **Customer Lifetime Value (CLTV)** predicts the total revenue you can expect from a customer throughout their relationship with your business, allowing you to focus on acquiring and retaining high-value customers.

Tracking KPIs regularly helps you spot trends early, so you're not blindsided by cash flow issues or shrinking profits.

3. Tools to Clear the Fog – Financial Software for the Rest of Us

If you're not a numbers person (and that's okay! I certainly wasn't when I had my first business), financial clarity can feel like learning calculus all over again. Fortunately, tools and apps make it easy. Think of them as your financial GPS—plug in the numbers, and they'll show you the way.

Some great options for non-financial folks:

- **QuickBooks Online**: The gold standard for small business accounting. It's like hiring a bookkeeper without the awkward small talk.
    - Start with the income and expense categories feature to understand where your money goes each month.
- **Xero**: Sleek, easy to use, and popular with e-commerce businesses.
    - Use the integration feature to sync with your bank account and get real-time transaction updates.
- **Wave**: A free alternative if you're just getting started and want to keep things lean.
    - Perfect if you're just starting; try the invoicing tool to streamline billing, even if you're on a budget.

These tools help automate the boring stuff—like invoicing and expense tracking—so you can spend more time on things that matter, like building your business or binge-watching your favorite show.

Real-World Example: Amazon's Early Struggles with Financial Clarity

Believe it or not, even the mighty Amazon didn't have its financial act together at the beginning. Jeff Bezos had grand ideas about building the "everything store," but for the first few years, the company was burning through cash faster than a bonfire at a music festival.

So how did they survive? By getting crystal clear on their finances. They focused on cash flow, adjusting spending, and raising capital at just the right times. Today, Amazon is a titan—but that wouldn't have happened if they'd ignored the numbers.

Another example is Peloton. They faced financial challenges as they grew, but by closely monitoring cash flow and profit margins, they adapted their model to shift from hardware sales to a subscription-based approach, achieving more predictable revenue.

On the other hand, consider the case of Toys "R" Us, a once-giant toy retailer that ultimately filed for bankruptcy. While there were multiple factors at play, a significant contributor was their struggle to manage debt and adapt to the changing retail landscape. They faced increasing competition from online retailers like Amazon, and their heavy debt burden hindered their ability to invest in e-commerce and innovate. This ultimately led to their downfall, highlighting the importance of staying vigilant about financial health and adapting to market changes.

Wrap-Up: Clarity Is Power (and It's Not That Scary)

Financial clarity isn't about becoming a CPA—it's about understanding enough to steer your business in the right direction. When you know what your numbers are saying, you make better decisions, avoid nasty surprises, and sleep better at night.

The Takeaways:

1. **Check your financials regularly.**
2. **Track a few key KPIs.**
3. **Use tools to make it easier.**

You don't need a finance degree—you just need a bit of focus, the right tools, and a dash of curiosity. And if things feel too overwhelming, that's what accountants are for. You've got this!

Now that you're armed with a better understanding of financial clarity, it's time to take action! Start by reviewing your latest financial statements. If you haven't already, consider implementing a user-friendly accounting software like QuickBooks Online or Xero to make tracking and analyzing your finances easier. And if you're feeling overwhelmed or unsure where to start, don't hesitate to reach out to a financial professional for guidance. Remember, every step you take towards understanding your numbers brings you closer to achieving your business goals.

Chapter 2: Profitability – The Art of Making Money (Not Just Revenue)

"Price is what you pay. Value is what you get." – Warren Buffett

This chapter is packed with practical advice, real-world examples, and a touch of humor. It'll help non-financial business owners understand the importance of profitability and avoid common pitfalls. Let me know what you think!

Introduction: Why Profit > Revenue

Revenue is cool. It's that big flashy number that looks impressive on paper, like having a million followers on Instagram. But here's the catch: Just like social media, if those followers don't engage, they're not doing much for you. In business terms, revenue without profit is like running on a treadmill—you're moving, but you're not really getting anywhere.

Profitability is where the magic happens. It's the difference between running a business and running a very expensive hobby. The goal isn't just to rack up sales but to make money from what you sell. This chapter will help you avoid the pitfalls of profitless growth and show you how to turn that revenue into real, spendable cash.

1. Profitless Growth: The Trap of Chasing Sales

It's tempting to think that more sales automatically mean more profit. But here's a reality check: Growth without profit is like filling a leaky bucket. You might be pouring in water (sales), but if your costs aren't under control, it all just drains away.

Many startups fall into this trap. Founders get excited about sales numbers and invest heavily in marketing, fancy office spaces, and product development—only to realize later that they're barely covering costs. If your costs grow faster than your revenue, you're in trouble.

Consider Netflix. During its rapid growth years, Netflix invested heavily in content production and technology infrastructure. Though subscribers increased, the company only turned a sustainable profit by meticulously balancing growth costs against profitability targets and cost efficiency.

Metaphor: Imagine opening a lemonade stand. You sell 100 cups for $1 each (yay!). But if lemons, sugar, and cups cost $1.50 per drink, congratulations—you've just scaled failure.

Common mistakes that reduce profitability, such as:

- **Over-Discounting**: Offering discounts without considering the effect on margins.
- **Ignoring Operational Inefficiencies**: Spending on unnecessary software, unoptimized processes, or excess inventory.
- **Focusing on Volume over Value**: Trying to grow too fast through low-margin products rather than focusing on high-value items.

A classic mistake is to over-discount in the hope of increasing sales. But if you're slashing prices, it's crucial to know how much profit you're giving away. Many retailers, for example, find themselves in a profit squeeze after launching a discount-heavy sales campaign without realizing how much it eats into their margins.

I hope you are starting to see the impact and the importance of watching margins and operating smartly.

2. Case Study: Tesla's Bumpy Road to Profitability

Tesla is now one of the most valuable companies in the world, but its journey was bumpy. For years, Elon Musk focused on building the future of electric cars, pouring billions into R&D, production, and infrastructure. While Tesla was raking in sales, they were also burning cash faster than a Tesla on Ludicrous Mode.

The problem? Tesla chased growth without initially managing costs effectively. It wasn't until Musk implemented strict cost-cutting measures—closing showrooms, reducing perks, and streamlining production—that Tesla started to see a profit.

Takeaway: Vision is essential, but so is financial discipline. Balance big dreams with a sharp focus on margins and costs.

3. E-Commerce Lessons: Revenue ≠ Profit

Let's shift to e-commerce, where businesses can easily fall into a similar trap. Many online businesses chase sales through discounts, free shipping, and paid ads—but without watching their margins, they end up barely breaking even (or worse, losing money).

Example:

You sell a trendy product for $50. But between production costs ($25), marketing spend ($15), and shipping ($10), you've wiped out any profit. Every sale leaves you with... exactly $0. And yet, sales seem to be booming!

The Solution? Manage Your Margins:

- **Know Your Numbers**: Track real costs—materials, ads, packaging, and shipping.
- **Strategic Pricing**: Avoid racing to the bottom with discounts. Instead, build a brand that lets you charge what your product is worth. Look at Apple—they rarely discount because they've established a brand people pay a premium for. Here are some pricing strategies that can improve profitability:
    - **Value-Based Pricing**: Pricing products based on the perceived value to the customer rather than the cost of goods.
    - **Psychological Pricing**: Using prices that end in .99 to increase conversion or creating price tiers that push customers toward a mid-level offering.
    - **Premium Pricing**: Establishing a higher price to create a perception of superior quality, especially when the brand's reputation supports it (like Apple's approach).
- **Rethink Free Shipping**: Roll shipping costs into the product price or set a minimum purchase threshold.

Amazon provides a great example here. They use strategic shipping fees and bundle products for Prime members to maximize average order values while offsetting shipping costs.

---

4. Profitability Metrics to Watch

Keeping an eye on a few key metrics will give you a deeper understanding of your profitability. Here are three metrics beyond Gross and Net Profit Margins that can provide valuable insights:

- **Contribution Margin**
  What it is: Contribution Margin measures how much profit is made from each sale after covering variable costs, like production and shipping.
  Why it matters: This metric helps you evaluate the profitability of

specific products or services. A high contribution margin means each sale adds significantly to profit, while a low margin could indicate the need to adjust pricing or reduce costs.
Formula: (Revenue - Variable Costs) ÷ Revenue

- **Operating Margin**
  What it is: Operating Margin looks at what's left after subtracting all operating expenses, giving a clearer view of day-to-day efficiency.
  Why it matters: This metric is a great indicator of how effectively your business is running. If your operating margin is low, it may be a sign to trim expenses or rethink your operational strategy.
  Formula: (Operating Income ÷ Revenue) × 100

  Every business is it's own snowflake (the good kind not the woke kind), but my heart starts to flutter when is an operating margin of 10-15%.

- **Return on Assets (ROA)**
  What it is: ROA measures how effectively you're using assets (like equipment, inventory, or property) to generate profit.
  Why it matters: A higher ROA means you're getting more bang for your buck from your assets. It's especially useful for businesses that rely heavily on equipment or inventory to generate sales.
  Formula: (Net Income ÷ Total Assets) × 100

These metrics can add layers to your profitability analysis, helping you see where your business shines and where you might need to make adjustments.

5. How to Know if Your Business Is Actually Profitable

Profitability can feel elusive, especially with multiple products or services. But it doesn't have to be complicated. Start with these three simple checks:

- **Gross Profit Margin**: This shows how much money you're keeping after covering the cost of goods sold (COGS).
  Formula: (Revenue – COGS) ÷ Revenue
  Example: A healthy margin depends on your industry, but 20-50% is generally solid.

- **Net Profit Margin**: Your "all-in" profit—the money left after all expenses (rent, salaries, ads, taxes).
  Formula: (Net Profit ÷ Revenue) × 100
  This figure tells you if your business is actually profitable or just treading water. *Note:* It's similar to Operating Margin, but it looks at profitability after *all* expenses have been deducted, even non-operating expenses, like interest and taxes.

- **Break-Even Point**: How much do you need to sell to cover your costs?
  Formula: Fixed Costs ÷ (Price per Unit – Variable Costs per Unit)
  This helps you gauge when you'll actually start making a profit. Even large companies, like Spotify, keep a close eye on break-even calculations for subscription-based services to inform their growth strategies.

---

6. Profit-Boosting Strategies You Can Start Today

Here are some quick wins to boost profitability without reinventing the wheel:

1. **Trim the Fat**: Audit expenses regularly. Are you still paying for that software you forgot about?
2. **Raise Prices (Gently)**: A small increase can often go unnoticed if you're delivering value. Think about Netflix—

small, incremental price increases have allowed them to stay competitive while investing in new content.

3. **Bundle and Upsell**: Offer product bundles or complementary services to increase average order value. Fast-food chains are a prime example—combos are profitable because they increase order size.

4. **Focus on Repeat Customers**: It's cheaper to keep an existing customer than to acquire a new one. Use email marketing and loyalty programs to keep customers coming back. Sephora's loyalty program, for instance, drives repeat purchases by offering rewards, exclusive discounts, and more.

5. **Get Smart with Ads**: Instead of throwing money at general ads, use retargeting to reach people who've already shown interest.

Wrap-Up: Profitability Is an Art—But You Can Master It

Profitability isn't just about making money—it's about keeping more of what you make. The goal is to grow smart, not just fast. Sure, revenue looks flashy, but profit is what keeps the lights on and your stress levels low.

Key Takeaway:

Don't chase revenue at the expense of profit. Focus on controlling costs, managing margins, and maximizing every sale. Every profitable decision you make today sets you up for long-term success.

Chapter 3: Cash Flow – Keeping the Lights On

"The best way to make a small fortune is to start with a large one and forget to pay attention to cash flow." – Anonymous

This chapter gives you a practical, approachable look at cash flow management while tying in modern trends like crypto and an inspiring example from Netflix. It wraps up with actionable advice and humor, helping non-financial business owners feel confident about managing their cash flow. Let me know if you love this one, too!

Introduction: The Heartbeat of Your Business

Think of cash flow as your **business's heartbeat.** When it's steady and strong, everything runs smoothly. Miss a few beats, though, and things get serious fast. Unlike profits, which look nice on paper, cash flow is what pays the bills, keeps the lights on, and makes sure payroll goes out on time.

You've probably heard, "Cash is king." **But in reality, cash flow is king, queen, and the entire royal family.** You can be profitable on paper and still run out of cash—because profits are potential, while cash flow is what keeps your business alive day to day.

Let's Bust Some Myths (before we start)

Myth #1: If I'm Profitable, Cash Flow is Fine
Reality: Profit doesn't mean you have money in the bank. Cash flow accounts for timing, while profit looks at totals.

Myth #2: More Sales Will Solve My Cash Flow Problems
Reality: Not if you're overspending or waiting too long to get paid. Sometimes more sales just mean bigger headaches.

Myth #3: Only Big Businesses Need to Worry About Cash Flow
Reality: Cash flow issues sink more small businesses than big ones. Keep an eagle eye on it from day one!

---

1. The Crypto Angle: New Tools, New Risks

Let's talk about cryptocurrency. A growing number of businesses—especially in e-commerce—are accepting crypto payments to speed up cash flow and cut payment processing fees. It sounds cool and futuristic, right? It is! But it also comes with risks.

- **The Good**: Payments through Bitcoin, Ethereum, or stablecoins can be instant, meaning you get cash (or rather, crypto) in real-time without waiting for banks to process transactions.
- **The Risk**: Crypto prices can fluctuate wildly—the $1,000 worth of Bitcoin you received yesterday might be worth $850 today. Ouch.
- **Solution**: Many companies use crypto payment processors like BitPay or Coinbase Commerce to convert crypto to cash immediately, reducing risk. But remember, this only makes sense if your customers want to pay in crypto. If not, stick with traditional currency for now.

To figure out if accepting crypto makes sense for *your* business, consider your target audience. Are they tech-savvy? Do they already use crypto? If so, offering crypto payments could give you a competitive edge and attract new customers. But if your customer base is less familiar with crypto, it might create more confusion than convenience. You can always start by accepting a popular stablecoin like USDC, which is pegged to the US dollar and less volatile than Bitcoin, Ethereum, or Shiba Inu. (Full disclosure, I own all three.)

Take a look at Overstock.com. They were one of the first major retailers to embrace Bitcoin, and it paid off. They attracted a new segment of crypto-enthusiast customers and saw a significant increase in sales. However, it's important to remember that Overstock caters to a tech-savvy audience. What works for them might not work for everyone.

The takeaway? Speed matters. The faster you collect cash, the more flexibility you have to cover expenses and reinvest in your business. Here's your checklist before your start:

- **Know Your Audience**: Do your customers want to pay with crypto, or will this just confuse them?
- **Understand Your Risks**: Can you handle the volatility of crypto, or should you stick to traditional currency?
- **Get Help If Needed**: Do you have a crypto payment processor (like BitPay or Coinbase Commerce) to handle conversions safely?

2. Netflix's Cash Flow Crisis: A Masterclass in Survival

Before Netflix became a streaming giant, it faced serious cash flow issues. In the early 2000s, they were burning through cash to grow their DVD rental business—buying DVDs, shipping them nationwide, and building a subscriber base. Expenses were piling up, and profitability was uncertain.

Netflix could have easily run out of cash and gone under. So, what did they do?

- **Creative Financing**: Netflix partnered with DVD manufacturers to get better deals on bulk orders.

- **Prepaid Memberships:** They introduced subscription plans, meaning customers paid upfront, giving Netflix a quick injection of cash.
- **Managing Payables:** Netflix negotiated with vendors to extend payment terms, giving them more breathing room.

By managing their cash flow creatively, Netflix bought themselves time to pivot toward streaming. The rest is history.

These strategies weren't just random moves; they were carefully calculated to address specific cash flow challenges. By partnering with DVD manufacturers, Netflix reduced the cost of acquiring DVDs, which freed up cash for other expenses. Prepaid memberships provided a predictable inflow of cash, allowing them to plan and invest with more confidence. And by negotiating longer payment terms with vendors, they could hold onto their cash for longer, giving them more flexibility to manage their finances.

Takeaway: Cash flow management isn't just about survival—it gives you the breathing room to innovate and grow.

---

3. The Cash Flow Cycle: Know It, Own It

Cash flow is simply the money moving in and out of your business. If more cash is coming in than going out, you're golden. If not, you're in trouble. To stay on top of cash flow, understand the three key stages:

1. **Operating Cash Flow:** This is day-to-day cash flow—customer payments, payroll, rent, and other regular expenses.
    1. **Keeping the lights on.**
2. **Investing Cash Flow:** Money spent on long-term investments, like equipment or software, and cash you get from selling assets.
    1. **For growth and big plans.**
3. **Financing Cash Flow:** Cash from loans or investors, and cash that goes out to repay debt or distribute dividends.
    1. **Debt, loans, and investor funds.**

Understanding how these three types of cash flow interact is crucial for managing your overall financial health.

For example, strong operating cash flow can provide the funds needed for investing activities, like upgrading your equipment or expanding your facilities. Or, if your operating cash flow is weak, you might need to rely on financing activities, like taking out a loan, to cover your expenses. By keeping a close eye on all three, you can get a holistic view of your cash flow situation and make informed decisions.

Keep an eye on all three, but especially on operating cash flow. Think of it as your business's pulse—if it's strong, everything else falls into place.

4. Use a Cash Flow Forecast: Your Crystal Ball

If cash flow is your heartbeat, a forecast is your stethoscope. It lets you spot issues before they become emergencies. A cash flow forecast helps you predict when cash will come in, when it will go out, and when you might need extra cash.

Creating a forecast is easier than it sounds:

- **Step 1**: List expected cash inflows—sales, payments from customers, loans, etc.
- **Step 2**: List expected cash outflows—rent, payroll, inventory, ads, and other expenses.
- **Step 3**: Track the difference to see if you're heading toward a positive or negative cash flow situation.

While a simple spreadsheet can be effective, there are also tools and software that can help you create more sophisticated forecasts. Some accounting software, like QuickBooks Online and Xero, include built-in forecasting features. You can also explore dedicated forecasting tools or even use AI-powered forecasting assistants to help you predict future cash flow with greater accuracy.

Common mistakes:

- **Overly Optimistic Sales Predictions:** Predicting next month's sales will double? Great for motivation, terrible for cash flow if it doesn't happen.
- **Ignoring Seasonality:** If sales slow in winter, don't pretend they won't. Stockpile cash in busy months.
- **Leaving Out Fixed Expenses:** Rent doesn't just disappear because you didn't write it in the forecast.

No need for fancy software! If you're a client, drop us an email at consultations@nealsongroup.com, and we'll send you a free cash flow template to get started.

5. Practical Cash Flow Hacks You Can Start Using Today

Here are five cash flow hacks to help keep the cash flowing steadily:

1. **Speed Up Receivables**: Send invoices immediately upon work completion, and offer early payment discounts.

   Offer a 2% discount for clients who pay within 10 days—it might seem small, but it works wonders for cash flow.

2. **Stretch Out Payables**: Pay vendors as close to the due date as possible—without harming relationships, of course.

   For example, pay your software subscriptions on the last day of the billing cycle. It's a small move, but it adds up.

3. **Inventory Management**: Don't let products sit on shelves. Forecast demand and keep inventory lean.

   If you sell coffee, stock up more beans before your busy season, but don't overstock milk, which can go bad.

4. **Plan for Seasonality**: If you know sales dip during certain months, build up cash reserves to get through the slow periods.

   Landscaping business? Save cash from summer for winter when work slows down.

5. **Use a Line of Credit**: Even if you don't need it now, having access to credit gives you a safety net for unexpected expenses.

   Set up a line of credit even if you don't need it immediately. For example, if you run a retail store, you can use it during the holiday season when you need to stock up on inventory, then pay it down when sales pick up. This way, you're not scrambling for cash or missing out on sales opportunities.

6. **Reduce unnecessary expenses:** Take a close look at your recurring expenses and identify areas where you can cut back. Maybe you can negotiate a lower rate on your internet service or find a more affordable supplier for your office supplies.

   Do a quick audit of your subscriptions. For example, if your team rarely uses a premium project management tool, consider switching to a free or lower-cost plan. Another idea: consolidate your software to platforms that do double duty, like using Zoom's free plan for team meetings instead of paying for multiple video conferencing tools.

7. **Offer recurring subscriptions:** If your business model allows for it, consider offering subscription-based services or products. This provides a predictable stream of recurring revenue, which can significantly improve your cash flow stability.

   If you own a pet supply store, offer a 'Pet of the Month' subscription box where customers receive a curated package each month. This way, you create predictable revenue, reduce the risk of unsold inventory, and build customer loyalty.

8. **Implement a robust credit policy:** To minimize the risk of late payments or bad debt, establish clear credit terms and follow up diligently on outstanding invoices. Consider offering incentives for early payments and implementing late payment penalties.

   Set clear terms in your invoices, like payment due in 30 days with a 1% late fee for overdue payments. You could also send automated reminders a week before the payment is due. For example, a landscaping business might offer a small discount for early payment or, conversely, charge a late fee for overdue accounts. These practices encourage timely payments and reduce cash flow gaps.

By implementing these suggestions, you can add depth and detail to your chapter while maintaining its engaging and informative style. You're doing a great job of making financial concepts accessible to non-financial business owners!

Wrap-Up: Cash Flow Is the Fuel That Powers Your Business

Here's the bottom line: Profit is nice, but cash flow keeps the lights on. You could be swimming in revenue, but if there's no cash in the bank, your business won't survive. By staying on top of your cash flow—whether through crypto, creative financing, or just a simple forecast—you give yourself the breathing room to innovate, grow, and stay ahead.

Key Takeaway:

1. **Forecast your cash flow.**
2. **Collect cash faster than you spend it.**
3. **Keep an eye on outflows—and stay vigilant.**

If it all feels overwhelming, remember—even Netflix struggled with cash flow. Look where they are now. You've got this!

Ready to give it a go?

Here's your Cash Flow Action Plan:

- *Step 1:* Set up a basic cash flow forecast—predict what's coming in and going out.
- *Step 2:* Identify one or two practical hacks (like speeding up receivables) and put them to work immediately.
- *Step 3:* Monitor your cash flow monthly. Adjust forecasts and strategies as needed.
- *Step 4:* Review your operating, investing, and financing cash flows every quarter to spot patterns and improvements.

C'mon you got this!

Chapter 4: Financial Planning – Setting Goals You Can Actually Hit

"Dreams without deadlines are just fairytales." - Judi Holler, from her book Fear Is My Homeboy.

This chapter shows how AI tools are making financial planning easier for businesses of all sizes. It emphasizes achievable goals and flexibility, ensuring the content stays relevant for e-commerce owners, crypto entrepreneurs, and HOA boards alike. Let me know if this hits the mark!

Introduction: Your Financial Plan Is a GPS (Not a Crystal Ball)

Imagine heading off on a cross-country road trip without a GPS or a map. You might eventually get where you want to go, but not without wrong turns, wasted time, and expensive detours. That's exactly what it's like running a business without a financial plan. You're moving, but with no idea if you're on the right path.

Here's the good news: Financial planning isn't about locking yourself into a rigid path. Think of it as setting a destination. Sure, you can take detours and change your route, but at least you know where you're going. This chapter will show you how to make budgeting and forecasting simple, effective, and even fun. Plus, we'll dive into how AI tools like ChatGPT are transforming business planning for e-commerce, cryptocurrency, and HOA ventures.

1. Budgeting Without the Boring Bits

"Budgeting" doesn't exactly scream excitement, but here's a secret: A good budget gives you freedom, not restrictions. When you know where your money is going, you can make smarter decisions without constantly worrying about running out of cash.

- **Example: E-commerce Inventory Planning**
  Let's say you run an online store selling unique, sustainable home goods. A budget helps you determine how much inventory to buy without getting stuck with leftover stock that doesn't sell. It also shows you how much to set aside for marketing—because if nobody knows about your products, nobody's buying them.

  For example, your budget might reveal that you're spending too much on paid advertising and not enough on email marketing. Or, it might show that you're overstocking certain products that aren't selling well. This allows you to make data-driven adjustments and allocate your resources more effectively.

- **Example: HOA Assessments**
  For HOAs, budgets are essential to prevent unexpected costs. No one wants to hear, "Surprise! We need to raise dues because we didn't plan for pool repairs." A clear budget helps HOA boards set realistic dues and build reserves for future maintenance—avoiding emergency assessments (and frustrated residents).

  A well-planned budget also helps HOA boards anticipate long-term maintenance needs. For instance, if you know the community pool will need major repairs in five years, you can start setting aside funds gradually to avoid a sudden increase in dues when the time comes.

- **Example: Crypto Business Operating Costs**
  In the crypto world, budgeting is crucial to cover unpredictable costs like security upgrades or transaction fees. A budget ensures you're setting aside enough for operations without dipping into funds needed for future growth.

  For instance, a crypto startup might budget for ongoing security audits, software development, and legal consultations to ensure compliance with evolving regulations. A budget helps prioritize these essential costs and avoid overspending on less critical areas.

Pro Tip: Your budget isn't carved in stone—it's a guide. Business is unpredictable, so adjust along the way rather than ignoring a shortfall while costs quietly stack up.

---

2. Forecasting: Predicting the Future (Sort of)

Forecasting sounds fancy, but really, it's just educated guessing based on your numbers and trends. It's like checking the weather before a road trip. Forecasting can't guarantee the outcome, but it helps you prepare for what's likely.

In business, a solid forecast tells you:

- When you'll have extra cash to reinvest in growth or inventory
- When you might hit a slow season and need to conserve funds
- When you may need outside funding to cover expenses or fuel expansion

AI in Action: This is where AI tools like ChatGPT shine. Business owners can now use AI to create financial forecasts, analyze market trends, and predict demand. Imagine being able to ask:

"Based on sales from the last 6 months, how much inventory should I order for December?"

AI tools analyze historical data faster than you can say "spreadsheet" and offer real-time recommendations, so you're always one step ahead. And the best part? No finance degree required.

But AI's capabilities go beyond just crunching numbers. It can also analyze external factors like market trends, economic indicators, and even social media sentiment to provide more nuanced and accurate forecasts. This helps you anticipate potential disruptions, identify emerging opportunities, and make proactive decisions rather than reacting to changes after they happen.

3. How AI Tools Are Changing Financial Planning

AI is no longer exclusive to tech giants. Small and medium-sized businesses across industries are using tools like ChatGPT and other forecasting platforms to make smarter, faster decisions.

For instance, tools like **PlanGuru** and **Adaptive Insights** offer powerful forecasting and budgeting capabilities specifically designed for businesses. E-commerce platforms like **Shopify** are increasingly integrating AI-powered forecasting tools to help sellers predict demand and optimize inventory. And in the crypto space, platforms like **CoinMetrics** and **Glassnode** provide advanced analytics and forecasting tools for traders and investors.

- **Scenario Planning**: Wondering how a 10% increase in marketing spend will impact cash flow? AI can run scenarios and provide answers in seconds.
- **Forecasting Sales Trends**: AI can analyze market data, seasonal trends, and customer behavior to predict when sales will spike or dip. This is essential for e-commerce businesses managing fluctuating inventory or crypto businesses anticipating transaction volumes.
- **Expense Optimization**: AI tools can identify patterns in expenses, suggesting where you can cut costs without sacrificing quality.

Imagine an HOA board using ChatGPT to ask, "How much should we set aside for pool maintenance next year based on similar projects nearby?" AI can analyze regional data and provide an accurate estimate, saving hours of research and guesswork.

In e-commerce, AI tools help sellers predict when to restock and by how much, reducing the risk of excess inventory. And for crypto businesses, AI can monitor volatility patterns and recommend transaction timing to optimize profitability.

And for crypto traders, AI can be a literal game-changer. Platforms like Augur use AI to analyze market sentiment and predict the outcome of future events. This allows traders to make more informed decisions about their investments, and potentially increasing their profits in such a highly speculative market.

NOTE: THIS IS NOT INVESTMENT ADVICE. Crypto trading is risky business. Don't come crying to me if you bet the farm on Dogecoin and end up living in a cardboard box. (Though, to be fair, that *would* make for an interesting chapter in my next book.)

---

4. Setting Goals You Can Actually Hit

Financial planning without goals is like driving in circles. You need clear, achievable milestones to measure progress and stay motivated. But here's the trick: Set goals you can actually hit.

Start with **SMART** goals:

- **Specific**: "Increase revenue by 10% in Q4" is better than "Make more money."
- **Measurable**: Track progress with monthly reports.
- **Achievable**: Aim for realistic growth based on your business's performance.
- **Relevant**: Make sure your goals align with your strategy.
- **Time-bound**: Set a deadline—without one, goals tend to drift.

Goal Example: E-commerce

- **Goal**: Increase average order value (AOV) by 15% in Q4.

- **How**: Offer bundles or free shipping on orders over a set amount.
- **Other**: Reduce customer churn by 5% by implementing a personalized email marketing campaign and offering loyalty rewards.

Goal Example: HOA

- **Goal**: Build a reserve fund of $50,000 by year-end.
- **How**: Allocate 10% of dues to reserves and reduce discretionary expenses.
- **Other**: Improve community engagement by increasing participation in social events by 20% through targeted communication and diverse event offerings.

Goal Example: Crypto Business

- **Goal**: Stabilize cash flow by reducing transaction costs by 10%.
- **How**: Implement transaction scheduling based on AI-driven predictions and use stablecoins for large transactions to avoid volatility.
- **Other**: Increase brand awareness by 30% by launching a content marketing strategy focused on educating potential customers about the benefits of your crypto product or service.

The key? Break big goals into smaller steps and celebrate small wins along the way—because hitting goals, no matter how small, feels great.

---

5. Keep It Simple and Stay Flexible

A solid financial plan keeps you focused but shouldn't feel like a ball and chain. Adjustments are normal—even expected. Maybe your e-commerce campaign outperforms expectations (fantastic!), or maybe unexpected HOA repairs pop up (not so fantastic). Either way, plans change, and that's okay.

Pro Tip: Schedule regular check-ins (monthly or quarterly) to review your plan. Are you on track? What's working? What needs adjustment?

The goal isn't perfection—it's progress.

Wrap-Up: Planning for Success, One Goal at a Time

Financial planning is about more than just numbers—it's about setting a direction and gaining confidence. With a clear plan, a bit of forecasting, and smart tools like AI, you'll know when to speed up, when to slow down, and when to adjust.

Here's the final takeaway:

1. **Set achievable goals.**
2. **Use a budget to guide spending—not restrict it.**
3. **Leverage AI tools to forecast trends and optimize decisions.**
4. **Stay flexible, and don't be afraid to pivot.**

So, take charge of your financial future. Set clear goals, create a flexible budget, and leverage the power of AI to make informed decisions. Remember, financial planning isn't about restricting your business; it's about empowering it to reach its full potential. With a well-crafted plan, you can navigate the road ahead with confidence and achieve the success you deserve.

And remember: Even if you take a few detours, with the right plan, you'll always find your way.

Chapter 5: Tools and Tech – Finance Doesn't Have to Be Hard

"Do what you do best and outsource the rest." – Peter Drucker

This chapter includes a relatable success story. The website references provides you with a starting point to explore further, and the Gymshark case study highlights the power of AI and tech for financial success. Hope you enjoy.

Introduction: There's an App for That—and Yes, It Will Make Your Life Easier

Gone are the days when managing business finances meant drowning in spreadsheets and receipts. Today, there's a tool for almost everything—budgeting, invoicing, payments, analytics, inventory management, and more. And the best part? Many of these tools are user-friendly and affordable, so you don't need an accounting degree to get started.

Think of financial tech as your business's sidekick—helping you stay organized, get paid on time, and even predict future trends. This chapter will dive into the best tools for managing your finances, explore how AI-powered analytics are transforming industries like e-commerce, cryptocurrency, and HOA management, and highlight why automating finance tasks is a game-changer for businesses of any size. By the end, you'll be equipped to run your business smarter, not harder.

1. Payment Tools That Get You Paid Faster

Every business owner knows that cash flow is king, and one of the easiest ways to improve it is by getting paid on time. Waiting on payments can cripple cash flow, especially if you're a small business or a startup. Here are some payment tools that make invoicing and collecting payments a breeze, ensuring you're paid quickly and efficiently:

- **Wave** (waveapps.com)
  Wave offers free invoicing and accounting software designed specifically for small businesses. You can send invoices, accept online payments, and track expenses—all in one place. It's a fantastic option for businesses just starting out or anyone looking to cut accounting costs. With automated reminders, Wave can help you follow up on unpaid invoices and improve your cash flow effortlessly.

  While Wave is free for invoicing and accounting, they do charge transaction fees for online payments. However, their fees are competitive with other processors, and the free software can be a significant cost-saver for small businesses.

- **Stripe** (stripe.com)
  Stripe is a powerhouse for e-commerce payments. It lets you accept a range of payment methods: credit cards, Apple Pay, Google Pay, and even cryptocurrency. Stripe's customizable checkout provides customers with a seamless payment experience, which is particularly useful for online businesses with a global reach. Stripe also offers fraud prevention tools and detailed analytics, so you're always in control of your payments and customer data.

  Stripe is known for its developer-friendly platform, making it a popular choice for businesses that want to customize their checkout experience or integrate payments with their own applications.

- **Square** (squareup.com)
  Square offers a variety of payment solutions for both online and in-person transactions. It's especially popular with small brick-and-mortar businesses for its easy-to-use point-of-sale (POS) system, which links directly to Square's invoicing and online payment systems. Square's flat-rate pricing is transparent, so you know exactly what to expect, whether you're processing a $5 transaction or a $5,000 one.

  Square also offers additional tools like employee management, payroll, and marketing features, making it a comprehensive platform for businesses that want to manage multiple aspects of their operations in one place.

- **Crypto Wallets (e.g., Coinbase Commerce)**
  Some businesses are joining the crypto bandwagon to offer alternative payment methods. With Coinbase Commerce, you can accept cryptocurrencies like Bitcoin, Ethereum, and Shiba Inu and convert them to cash right away. While crypto is still a niche payment method, accepting it could help your business stand out with tech-savvy customers. For instance, crypto businesses can use wallets like MetaMask or Trust Wallet to manage and transfer digital assets.

  It's important to research and choose a reputable crypto wallet provider with strong security measures to protect your digital assets. Consider factors like transaction fees, ease of use, and customer support when making your selection.

Automation isn't just about convenience; it's about accuracy and efficiency. By automating tasks like invoice generation, payment reminders, and expense tracking, you reduce the risk of human error and free up your time to focus on more strategic aspects of your business.

Look for tools that integrate seamlessly with each other. For example, your accounting software should ideally connect with your payment processor, your CRM system, and your e-commerce platform. This creates a centralized hub for your financial data and streamlines your workflow.

If you use QuickBooks Online, you can connect it to platforms like Stripe or PayPal for payment processing, Shopify for e-commerce, and HubSpot for CRM. This allows for smooth data flow and eliminates the need for manual data entry.

Pro Tip: If your business model involves regular customer billing (such as subscription services), look into automated payment tools like Recurly or Chargebee, which specialize in recurring billing and subscription management.

2. Accounting Software to Keep You Organized

Accounting is often one of the most time-consuming parts of running a business. But with the right accounting software, you can automate tasks, save time, and reduce human error. Here are a few top options:

- **QuickBooks Online** (quickbooks.intuit.com)
  QuickBooks is the gold standard in small business accounting. It's a full-suite platform that offers invoicing, expense tracking, payroll, and tax management. QuickBooks integrates with your bank, so your transactions update automatically. It's a powerful tool that can handle most of your accounting needs, and it scales with your business, meaning you won't outgrow it quickly.

- **Xero** (xero.com)
  Xero is particularly popular with e-commerce and crypto businesses due to its inventory tracking and seamless integrations with platforms like Shopify, Stripe, and Coinbase. Xero is known for its intuitive design and user-friendly interface, making it a good choice for business owners who want a clean, easy-to-navigate platform that also packs a punch.

- **FreshBooks** (freshbooks.com)
  FreshBooks is an invoicing and accounting tool that's especially favored by freelancers, consultants, and service-based businesses. FreshBooks makes invoicing simple and allows you to track time and expenses. If you're a solopreneur or running a small service-based business, FreshBooks could be the perfect fit.

Pro Tip: When selecting accounting software, check if it integrates with other tools you're already using. This can simplify things immensely by linking your entire financial ecosystem together, allowing data to flow automatically across platforms.

Imagine this: a customer places an order on your Shopify store. The order details automatically flow into Xero, generating an invoice and updating your inventory levels. Once the customer pays through Stripe, the payment is recorded in Xero, reconciling with your bank account and updating your financial reports. This seamless flow of information saves you countless hours of manual data entry and reduces the risk of errors.

3. Analytics Tools: The Power of Knowing Your Numbers

In today's data-driven world, understanding your numbers is crucial. Thanks to AI-powered analytics, you can now track margins, trends, and forecasts in real-time. Whether you're running an e-commerce site, a crypto enterprise, or an HOA, these tools provide insights that drive better decision-making.

- **Google Analytics** (analytics.google.com)
  Google Analytics is essential for any online business. It helps you track website performance and understand customer behavior. E-commerce sites can see where visitors come from, which pages they visit, and which products are top sellers. You can use this information to optimize your sales funnel, identify high-value pages, and improve your conversion rate. For crypto

or niche e-commerce businesses, these insights are valuable for adjusting marketing strategies.

Google Analytics also offers advanced features like conversion tracking, which allows you to measure the effectiveness of your marketing campaigns and identify which channels are driving the most valuable traffic to your site.

- **Tableau** (tableau.com)
  Tableau takes data visualization to the next level, allowing you to create detailed dashboards and interactive charts. Use it to track financial KPIs, spot trends, and identify growth opportunities. Many businesses use Tableau to forecast demand and manage cash flow. Imagine how powerful it is to visualize your cash flow over time or identify the most profitable product lines visually.

  While Tableau is a powerful tool, it can have a steeper learning curve than some other analytics platforms. However, they offer extensive training resources and a supportive community to help users get up to speed.

- **Zoho Analytics** (zoho.com/analytics)
  Zoho Analytics is a great option for small businesses wanting a robust analytics tool without breaking the bank. It integrates with many popular apps like Shopify, QuickBooks, and even social media platforms, making it easy to pull all your data into one place. Zoho Analytics allows you to run sales, revenue, and customer analysis, helping you uncover valuable insights about your business.

  Zoho Analytics also offers AI-powered features like anomaly detection, which can automatically identify unusual patterns in your data, alerting you to potential issues or opportunities.

Pro Tip: Use AI-powered analytics platforms to simplify data interpretation. Tools like IBM Watson Analytics and Microsoft Power BI can help you identify trends and correlations without a data science degree. This allows you to make quick, data-driven decisions to grow your business.

4. Inventory Management Tools: Never Run Out of Stock (or Overload It)

For e-commerce and product-based businesses, inventory management is crucial. Poor inventory control can lead to missed sales opportunities or excess stock that sits unsold.

- **TradeGecko** (tradegecko.com)
  TradeGecko (now part of QuickBooks Commerce) is ideal for small and medium-sized e-commerce businesses. It syncs inventory, orders, and sales across channels, so you can manage all aspects of your product-based business in one place. You can also integrate it with Shopify, Amazon, and other major platforms.

- **ShipBob** (shipbob.com)
  ShipBob is a third-party logistics provider that handles fulfillment for e-commerce companies. ShipBob's software lets you monitor your inventory in real-time and tracks orders as they move through the fulfillment process. This level of insight is essential if you're managing a high volume of orders and want to avoid stockouts or overstock issues.

- **InventoryLab** (inventorylab.com)
  InventoryLab is popular among Amazon FBA sellers for its inventory management and profitability tracking. It provides a real-time view of inventory performance and calculates profitability per item, so you know what's working and what's not.

Pro Tip: AI-driven inventory forecasting tools like Forecastly can analyze historical sales data to predict demand more accurately, so you never have to guess on reorders.

5. AI-Powered Success Story: Gymshark's Rise to the Top

Gymshark, the popular athletic wear brand, is a prime example of how AI-powered analytics can take a business to the next level. What began as a small fitness apparel company exploded into a global brand, partly due to their innovative use of AI and data analytics.

Gymshark used AI tools to:

- **Track Sales and Inventory in Real-Time**: Ensuring popular products stayed in stock and slow-moving inventory was managed appropriately.
- **Optimize Marketing Campaigns**: By analyzing customer behavior, Gymshark tailored ads to specific audiences, maximizing ad spend and improving targeting.
- **Forecast Demand for New Launches**: Using predictive analytics, they gauged demand for new products, reducing the risk of overstocking or missing out on high demand.

Gymshark's success demonstrates that AI isn't just about automating tasks; it's about gaining a deeper understanding of your customers and your business. By leveraging AI-powered analytics, they were able to identify trends, personalize their marketing efforts, and optimize their operations, ultimately leading to significant growth and profitability.

This data-driven approach allowed Gymshark to scale rapidly while maintaining healthy profit margins and efficient operations. The lesson here? Smart tools give you a competitive edge, and AI-driven insights aren't just for big companies anymore.

---

6. How to Choose the Right Tools for Your Business

With so many tools out there, choosing the right one can feel overwhelming. Here's a framework to help you pick the tools that fit your needs best:

1. **Start Small**: Choose tools that solve your biggest pain points first. If invoicing takes forever, start with a tool like Wave. If payments are delayed, try Stripe.
2. **Look for Integrations**: Pick tools that integrate with your current tech stack. For example, if you're already using Shopify, Xero and TradeGecko are seamless options.
3. **Consider Scalability**: Choose tools that will grow with your business. You don't want to outgrow your software in six months, which can result in unnecessary costs and data migration headaches.
4. **Take Advantage of Free Trials**: Many platforms offer free trials—test them out before committing. This is the best way to see if a tool is user-friendly, fits your workflow, and adds real value.

When implementing new financial tools and technologies, it's crucial to prioritize security and data privacy. Ensure that the tools you choose comply with relevant regulations like GDPR (General Data Protection Regulation) and CCPA (California Consumer Privacy Act). Look for features like data encryption, two-factor authentication, and regular security updates to protect your sensitive financial information.

Wrap-Up: Work Smarter, Not Harder

Technology has leveled the playing field for businesses of all sizes. Whether you're running an e-commerce store, managing an HOA, or growing a crypto enterprise, the right tools can save you time, reduce stress, and improve your bottom line. And the best part? Many of these tools are affordable—or even free.

Here's the plan:

1. **Choose one or two tools to try this week.**
2. **Use AI-powered analytics to keep an eye on margins and trends**.
3. **Experiment with automation to free up more time for the parts of your business you love.**

Finance doesn't have to be hard—with the right tools, it can be easy. Give them a try, and your business (and your sanity) will thank you!

Chapter 6: Building a Financial Strategy – Your Roadmap to Freedom

"If you don't design your own life plan, chances are you'll fall into someone else's plan. And guess what they have planned for you? Not much." – Jim Rohn

This chapter ties everything together, providing actionable steps and insights from Airbnb's pandemic pivot. It emphasizes the importance of setting goals, staying flexible, and asking for help.

Introduction: Financial Strategy Is Your GPS for Long-Term Success

Let's get one thing clear—you don't need to be a financial wizard to build a solid strategy. All you need is a basic understanding of your financials, clear goals, and the humility to ask for help when you need it. Think of a financial strategy as a roadmap that aligns your long-term vision with the reality of your numbers. It shows where you're going and how you'll get there, whether you're an HOA planning for major repairs, an e-commerce business preparing for holiday spikes, or a crypto business navigating a rapidly changing market.

Without a strategy, you're flying blind. While you might survive month-to-month, real financial freedom comes from planning ahead, making smart decisions, and sticking to your goals (with a few detours, of course). Let's dig into how to create a financial strategy that prepares you for long-term success and keeps you grounded through 2025 and beyond.

---

1. The Foundation: Aligning Goals with Financial Clarity, Profitability, and Cash Flow

By now, you've learned that **clarity, profitability, and cash flow** are the *holy trinity of business success*. Your strategy needs to connect all three so you're not just making money—you're keeping it and using it wisely. This foundation is critical, particularly as we move into a year with more focus on financial agility and strategic spending.

- **Financial Clarity**
  Your strategy starts with knowing where you stand. Regular financial reports give you the data you need to make confident decisions. Without clarity on reserves, for example, an HOA might face a financial crisis if they suddenly need a costly repair. A thorough understanding of your financials helps you avoid surprise costs and enables strategic adjustments when necessary.

  Real-World Example: Let's say you're a digital marketing firm. Financial clarity means knowing the real return on each marketing campaign—recognizing which ones bring in profits and which just add to your expenses. In 2023, The North Face took a highly strategic approach to its marketing spend, doubling down on sustainable practices and targeting campaigns based on performance data, which ultimately drove more cost-effective, profitable campaigns.

  By analyzing their campaign data, they might discover that social media ads are generating a higher return on investment than traditional print advertising. This insight could lead them to reallocate their budget and focus on the most effective channels.

- **Profitability**
  Revenue alone doesn't guarantee success. You need to focus on

profit margins, identifying which products or services bring in the most profit and eliminating those that are just breaking even. For instance, an e-commerce store might shift focus to high-margin products instead of chasing volume with low-cost items that barely cover expenses.

Example: Tesla, which initially struggled to bring down the costs of electric vehicles, was eventually able to improve profitability through more efficient manufacturing processes. By targeting higher-margin luxury models like the Model S before releasing more affordable options, Tesla grew profitably while continuing to innovate.

This strategy allowed them to establish a strong brand presence in the luxury market while generating the revenue needed to invest in research and development for more affordable models.

- **Cash Flow**
  Even profitable businesses can stumble if cash isn't available when bills are due. Your strategy should include cash flow forecasts to ensure you're never caught off guard. Planning ahead for seasonality—such as building a reserve fund during peak months to cover slower periods—keeps operations running smoothly without financial stress.

  Example: Many restaurants, especially those in tourist-heavy areas, have seen how important cash flow management can be. A restaurant in Miami, for example, may build a reserve during the high winter season to cover expenses during the summer slowdown, ensuring it has sufficient funds to pay bills and staff regardless of seasonal variations.

  This proactive approach to cash flow management helps them maintain stability during slower months and avoid layoffs or service disruptions.

When you understand your finances, you're not just reading numbers; you're gaining insights into the very heart of your business. You can identify what's working well, what needs improvement, and where to focus your energy for the greatest impact. This knowledge empowers you to make informed decisions, navigate challenges with confidence, and ultimately achieve your business goals.

By connecting your goals to these three pillars, you'll have a clearer sense of direction. You'll know when to invest, when to save, and when to pull back—without relying on guesswork.

2. Case Study: Airbnb's Pandemic Pivot – A Masterclass in Strategic Thinking

Airbnb's story offers a masterclass in strategic pivoting. Before the pandemic, Airbnb's model was simple: connect travelers with short-term rental hosts. Business was booming, and growth seemed unstoppable.

Then COVID-19 hit, and travel came to a halt. Airbnb's core business model was suddenly rendered useless. Many companies would have panicked, but Airbnb regrouped and strategically pivoted. Here's what they did:

- **Doubling Down on Long-Term Rentals**
  With remote work on the rise, there was increased demand for month-to-month rentals in desirable locations like beach towns and scenic countryside spots. Airbnb capitalized on this trend and began marketing to people seeking longer stays.
- **Cutting Costs**
  Airbnb made tough decisions, letting go of office space and pausing unnecessary projects to keep cash in the bank.
- **Focusing on Core Strengths**
  Instead of launching new products, Airbnb refined their platform to make hosting safer and easier, maintaining user trust and loyalty.

Airbnb also introduced 'Online Experiences' to cater to people stuck at home. These virtual experiences, hosted by experts and local guides, allowed people to connect and learn new skills, generating a new revenue stream for the company and providing hosts with alternative income opportunities

The result? Airbnb stayed afloat and bounced back stronger. When travel resumed, they were ready.

The takeaway? Strategic thinking isn't about predicting the future—it's about having the flexibility to pivot. A solid financial strategy gives you the freedom to adapt to changing conditions without losing sight of long-term goals.

3. Building a Financial Strategy That Works for You

Building a financial strategy may sound intimidating, but it's about connecting where you are today with where you want to be tomorrow.

Step 1: Set SMART Goals

SMART goals (mentioned in chapter 4) are essential because they provide a foundation to keep you grounded and focused. When setting goals, consider both short-term and long-term objectives. Short-term goals might focus on increasing sales or reducing expenses in the next quarter, while long-term goals might involve expanding into new markets or launching new products in the next few years.

- **Specific**: Know exactly what you're aiming for (e.g., grow revenue by 10%).
- **Measurable**: Track progress with regular financial reports.
- **Achievable**: Set realistic goals that won't set you up for failure.
- **Relevant**: Align your goals with your business model and financial health.
- **Time-bound**: Set deadlines to work toward.

Example: Peloton set specific goals around subscription growth rather than just product sales, helping it secure a stable revenue stream from its loyal customer base. Similarly, an e-commerce business might aim to increase average order value (AOV) by 15% in Q4 by bundling products or offering incentives for higher spending.

Step 2: Build a Cash Reserve

Life happens. Your strategy should include an emergency fund for unexpected expenses or seasonal slowdowns. A good rule of thumb is to set aside 3-6 months of operating expenses to ensure you're prepared for the unexpected.

The ideal size of your cash reserve will depend on factors like your industry, business model, and risk tolerance. Businesses with unpredictable revenue streams or high operating expenses may need a larger reserve than those with stable and predictable income.

Example: An unexpected HVAC breakdown in the middle of summer can be costly for an office or property. Having a cash reserve prevents these emergencies from becoming financial crises.

Step 3: Use Forecasting Tools to Stay Ahead

Forecasting is about spotting trends early and adjusting your plans before things go sideways. Tools like Xero, QuickBooks, and Google Sheets help you create forecasts, and AI-powered tools like ChatGPT provide fast insights. You might ask:

"How will a 5% increase in shipping costs impact my profit margins?"

Using AI tools allows you to adapt quickly to changes in expenses, customer behavior, or other variables, keeping your strategy flexible and relevant.

Forecasting can also help you identify potential risks and opportunities. For example, if your forecast predicts a cash shortage in a few months, you can take proactive steps to secure funding or adjust your spending. Or, if your forecast shows strong growth potential, you can confidently invest in expansion or new initiatives.

Step 4: Review and Adjust Regularly

Even the best strategies need regular adjustments. Schedule monthly or quarterly reviews to make sure you're on track. Assess what's working, what isn't, and be ready to tweak your goals. A successful financial strategy should evolve as your business grows and changes.

It's also important to involve key stakeholders in the review process. This could include your team members, financial advisors, or mentors. Gathering diverse perspectives can help you identify blind spots and make more informed adjustments to your strategy.

4. YO…..You Don't Have to Do It Alone

Here's a truth that every successful business owner knows: You don't have to be a financial genius, and you don't have to do it all yourself. That's why accountants, financial advisors, and consultants exist. The smartest business owners aren't those who try to do everything themselves—they're the ones who know when to ask for help.

If all this talk about financial strategy feels overwhelming, take a deep breath. Asking for help isn't a sign of weakness; it's a sign that you're serious about success. Outsourcing your financial strategy or seeking advice can save you time, stress, and potentially costly mistakes.

Think of it like this: even the most skilled athletes have coaches to guide them and help them improve. Similarly, even the most successful business owners can benefit from the expertise of financial professionals. They can provide objective insights, identify potential pitfalls, and help you develop a strategy that aligns with your unique business goals.

Wrap-Up: Your Roadmap to Financial Freedom

A well-built financial strategy gives you clarity, control, and confidence. It aligns your long-term goals with your finances, ensuring you stay profitable and cash-flow positive, even when life throws curveballs.

Key Takeaways

1. **Set clear, actionable goals**: SMART goals give you direction and keep you focused.

2. **Prioritize cash flow and profitability**: Stay on top of these to keep your business healthy.
3. **Prepare to pivot**: Flexibility allows you to adapt to unexpected changes.
4. **Ask for help when needed**: Even the best business owners rely on experts.

With a strong financial strategy in place, you'll have the freedom to grow your business, take calculated risks, and enjoy the journey— without constantly worrying about the next financial surprise.

Conclusion: Your Journey to Financial Freedom Starts Now!

Congratulations! You've made it through the entire book and are now equipped with the financial knowledge to navigate your business with confidence. You've learned how to gain clarity, boost profitability, manage cash flow, plan effectively, leverage technology, and build a winning financial strategy.

But remember, you don't have to do it alone. Running a business is challenging, and sometimes it's easier with a financial expert in your corner. If you need help with any aspect of your financial journey – from setting up cash flow forecasts to building a comprehensive strategy – The Nealson Group is here to support you.
We can help you with:
- Setting up a cash flow forecast
- Building a financial strategy tailored to your goals
- Managing your accounting
- Navigating tax planning
- Or simply making sense of it all

Just call us at 561.299.1020 or email consultations@nealsongroup.com to request a callback. We'll walk with you every step of the way because financial success isn't just about knowing the rules; it's about having the right support to make it happen.

Now, it's time to take massive action! Whether you start small by building a budget or dive headfirst into creating a financial strategy, keep moving forward. You have everything you need to take control of your business and unlock the freedom you deserve.

Remember: Success isn't about going it alone; it's about knowing when to ask for help. So, are you ready to make your financial goals a reality? We're here whenever you need us. Let's make it happen!"

Bonus Chapters:

Bonus Chapter 1: The People Factor – Unlocking Profit with Employee Engagement

"Clients do not come first. Employees come first. If you take care of your employees, they will take care of the clients." – Richard Branson

This bonus chapter ties together profitability, strategy, and practical business advice, giving you one more way to maximize your financial potential. It's actionable, relatable, and reinforces the idea that great businesses are built on great teams. Enjoy, you earned it.

Introduction: The Secret Weapon to Profit Isn't a New Tool—it's Your Team

When we talk about profitability, the first things that come to mind are product margins, sales, and cost control. But there's an essential ingredient often overlooked: people. Your employees are the heartbeat of your business, and when they're happy, engaged, and productive, everyone wins.

Here's the kicker: employee engagement isn't just about warm and fuzzy feelings—it's a powerful driver of profit. Studies show that companies with highly engaged employees are up to 21% more profitable than those without. Why? Engaged employees work harder, stick around longer, and create better outcomes. In short, a happy team = a profitable team. In this chapter, we'll explore the financial impact of engagement and provide real-world examples of businesses that have leveraged employee commitment to fuel their success.

1. Profit per Employee: What It Is and Why It Matters

Profit per employee is a valuable metric that sheds light on how efficiently a business generates income with its workforce. It's calculated simply by dividing your net profit by the number of employees:

Profit per Employee = Net Profit ÷ Number of Employees

This metric is relevant not only to tech giants but to businesses of all sizes. Understanding profit per employee can help you gauge your company's efficiency and highlight where adjustments in engagement or productivity could increase profitability.

Real-World Example: Apple

Apple, one of the most profitable companies globally, generates over $400,000 in profit per employee. This isn't just due to high product prices; it's because Apple is strategic about utilizing every team member. Through clear goal-setting, a culture of innovation, and support for employee growth, Apple maximizes productivity and engagement, resulting in a high return on each employee.

How Small Businesses Can Boost Profit per Employee

You don't need Apple's resources to improve profit per employee. Even small changes—like enhancing employee engagement, efficiency, and retention—can significantly impact your profitability.

2. The Cost of Disengagement: Why It's Expensive to Ignore Your People

Disengaged employees are like a leaky faucet. The damage isn't always immediate, but over time, disengagement drains your resources. A disengaged employee costs a company approximately 18% of their annual salary in lost productivity alone. Multiply that across your workforce, and you have a serious profitability problem.

Real-World Example: Zappos

Zappos, the online retailer known for its exceptional customer service, realized early on that happy employees lead to happy customers, which in turn boosts profits. Zappos built a culture of engagement by empowering employees to solve customer problems creatively, fostering flexibility, and recognizing great work. The result? Higher retention, lower turnover costs, and a skyrocketing level of customer loyalty that cemented Zappos as a beloved brand.

Lesson: Investing in employee engagement isn't just about making work enjoyable—it's a solid financial strategy.

3. Empowering Employees to Act: The Ritz-Carlton Model

One of the most inspiring examples of employee empowerment is The Ritz-Carlton. Known for its world-class customer service, The Ritz-Carlton trusts employees with the autonomy to make customer-focused decisions, empowering them to resolve guest issues without delay. Each employee has the discretion to spend up to $2,000 per guest to resolve complaints or enhance the guest experience. This approach is bold, but it allows Ritz-Carlton staff to create memorable experiences for guests and reinforces the hotel's luxury brand.

Financial Impact

While $2,000 might sound like a lot, consider the cost of a single disgruntled customer. Negative reviews or word-of-mouth complaints can deter future business. By empowering employees to "wow" guests, The Ritz-Carlton minimizes these potential costs and fosters repeat business. This commitment to service turns a potential expense into a long-term investment in brand loyalty.

4. Practical Steps to Boost Profit Per Employee

Improving employee engagement doesn't have to involve extravagant perks. Here are some effective ways to foster engagement, increase productivity, and ultimately boost profitability.

Step 1: Set Clear Goals (and Celebrate Wins)

Employees want to feel they're making a difference. Setting clear, achievable goals and celebrating wins, no matter how small, can make employees feel valued and motivated. When your team understands their impact on the company's success, they'll work more effectively.

Real-World Example: LinkedIn
LinkedIn practices goal transparency with quarterly and annual objectives that are accessible to all employees. Each team member understands their contribution to the broader company goals, which keeps them engaged and connected to LinkedIn's success.

Step 2: Offer Flexibility Where You Can

The post-pandemic world has shown us that flexible work arrangements are here to stay. Offering remote or hybrid work options, flexible hours, or even "no meeting" days can increase engagement without adding costs.

Real-World Example: Shopify
Shopify has implemented a "digital by default" approach, allowing employees to work remotely and giving them the flexibility to adapt their schedules. This shift has led to a happier, more productive workforce, with employees who feel trusted and valued.

Step 3: Provide Growth Opportunities

No one wants to feel stuck in a dead-end job. Offering growth opportunities—like workshops, mentorship programs, or online courses—keeps employees engaged by showing them a future with your company.

Real-World Example: Netflix
Netflix encourages employees to own their projects and offers freedom to pursue innovative ideas. This culture of autonomy and growth

attracts top talent and keeps them productive and committed.

Step 4: Conduct Stay Interviews

Understanding what keeps employees engaged is crucial. "Stay interviews" are informal conversations with employees about their experience, goals, and potential areas of improvement. They provide insight into what's working and what's not, allowing you to address concerns before they lead to disengagement or turnover.

Quick Tip: Regular stay interviews can prevent expensive turnover, uncover growth opportunities, and boost retention.

5. Retention: The Profitability Booster You Didn't Know You Needed

Replacing an employee can cost up to twice their annual salary, considering recruitment, onboarding, and the lost productivity that accompanies turnover. High turnover doesn't just hurt team morale; it's a profit killer. On the other hand, businesses with high retention rates save money and foster a positive work environment where employees feel valued.

Real-World Example: Southwest Airlines
Southwest Airlines boasts one of the highest retention rates in the airline industry. By cultivating a culture of employee appreciation and promoting from within, Southwest builds loyalty and reduces turnover. Employees feel secure, valued, and more committed to the company's long-term success, which translates into outstanding customer service and financial stability.

Quick Win: Conduct regular "pulse checks" with your team to gauge job satisfaction, understand potential frustrations, and address concerns before they escalate.

6. Profit-Boosting Engagement Strategies for Small Businesses

If you're thinking, "This all sounds great, but I run a small team—does this really matter?" the answer is yes. In small businesses, every team member plays a critical role, and disengagement can be especially damaging. For example, in a 5-person team, one disengaged person means 20% of your workforce is operating below capacity.

Engaged employees in small businesses are more likely to go the extra mile, solve problems creatively, and contribute to growth in meaningful ways. Here are some engagement strategies particularly suited to small teams:

Strategy 1: Encourage Cross-Training

In small businesses, versatility is invaluable. Cross-training employees to handle multiple roles builds flexibility and keeps employees engaged by allowing them to broaden their skill sets. This approach also prevents burnout, as employees can switch tasks and take on fresh challenges.

Example: A small bakery might train staff to work both front-of-house and in the kitchen. This flexibility not only boosts engagement but ensures coverage during busy times.

Strategy 2: Create a Culture of Recognition

A "thank you" goes a long way. Recognizing achievements and hard work builds a culture of appreciation and respect.

Example: At Buffer, a social media management tool, employees receive public recognition on a "Gratitude Wall," where team members can post thank-you notes to colleagues. This public appreciation reinforces team cohesion and motivates employees.

Strategy 3: Foster a Sense of Ownership

Small businesses thrive when employees feel they're directly contributing to the company's success. Encourage team members to bring ideas, suggest improvements, and take ownership of projects.

Example: Patagonia empowers employees by integrating environmental values into their work. Team members feel part of a larger mission, which drives engagement, productivity, and retention.

---

7. Real-World Success Story: The Impact of Employee Engagement at Trader Joe's

Trader Joe's is a prime example of how employee engagement can drive profitability. Known for exceptional customer service, Trader Joe's puts significant effort into training, engaging, and empowering its employees. Crew members are encouraged to "bring their personalities to work" and make personalized recommendations to customers, creating a memorable shopping experience.

The Financial Impact
Trader Joe's employees are so engaged that the company has lower turnover and higher customer satisfaction rates compared to competitors. These elements create a loyal customer base that returns not just for the products, but for the experience—a profitable strategy that leads to strong sales per square foot, often surpassing other grocery stores.

Lesson: Engaged employees can transform customer experiences and drive profitability in even the most competitive industries.

---

8. The Ritz-Carlton and Empowering Employees to Act

As we discussed, The Ritz-Carlton sets the standard for employee empowerment in customer service. With the freedom to spend up to $2,000 per guest to resolve issues or enhance experiences, Ritz-Carlton employees are trusted to make decisions that improve customer satisfaction. This trust is a major reason why Ritz-Carlton guests are so loyal.

Financial Insight

The costs of these guest-focused expenditures are far outweighed by the value of loyal repeat customers and positive word-of-mouth advertising. By empowering employees, The Ritz-Carlton has built a brand synonymous with luxury and exceptional service, illustrating how engagement can elevate a business and boost profitability.

Wrap-Up: The People Factor—Your Secret to Profitability

At the end of the day, your employees are your greatest asset. Investing in them doesn't just improve morale—it boosts productivity, reduces turnover, and increases profitability. If you want to unlock profit potential, focus on getting the most out of the team you already have.

Final Takeaways:

1. **Set clear goals and celebrate wins.**
2. **Offer flexibility and growth opportunities.**
3. **Invest in retention—it's cheaper than hiring.**
4. **Empower employees to act in customer-facing roles.**

You don't need to be a financial wizard to unlock profit with employee engagement. Simply care about your people, support their growth, and set them up for success.

Bonus Chapter 2: Taxes and Regulations in the Age of E-commerce, AI, and Cryptocurrency

"In this world, nothing is certain except death and taxes." – Benjamin Franklin

This chapter provides real-world examples, practical tools, and actionable advice to help you understand how tax regulations impact e-commerce, AI, and crypto businesses. Clarity and strategy lead to success, and The Nealson Group is your trusted guide in this ever-evolving digital space.

Introduction: Taxes? Yes. But We'll Make It Easy

Taxes aren't usually the fun part of running a business, especially in e-commerce or the crypto world. They bring unique complexities that can feel overwhelming, particularly when you're dealing with regulations around AI-driven technologies or decentralized finance. But don't worry—this chapter breaks down how you can navigate tax implications in a way that's manageable and clear, no matter how tech-forward your business is.

1. E-commerce Sales Tax Laws – What You Need to Know

The e-commerce landscape was forever changed by the 2018 Supreme Court decision in *South Dakota v. Wayfair*, which gave states the authority to require e-commerce businesses to collect sales tax even without a physical presence. In addition, AI-driven sales tracking tools are evolving, helping businesses anticipate where they might cross state tax thresholds based on customer trends and purchase volumes.

This is more than just a new rule; it's the kind of trend that calls for proactive adaptation. **Ask yourself, in five years, will the world be more or less digital?** If your answer is "more," you can't afford to ignore these changes. With automation, AI tools, and a good tax advisor, you can handle these challenges efficiently.

Key Points:

- **Nexus Requirements**: If your sales exceed certain thresholds (like $100,000 or 200 transactions) in any state, you'll need to collect sales tax.
- **Marketplace Platforms**: Platforms like Amazon and Shopify often manage sales tax for you but don't let this lull you into a false sense of security. Monitoring states where you file is still your responsibility.
- **Local Sales Tax Rates**: Some states apply additional local taxes, so your tax obligations might vary within the same state. AI-driven tools are now available to help manage this complexity in real time.

Beyond nexus requirements, it's also crucial to understand the specific product taxability rules in each state. Some states have exemptions for certain goods, like groceries or clothing, while others may have different tax rates for different product categories. Keeping track of these varying rules can be complex, but tools like Avalara and TaxJar can automate this process and ensure you're collecting the correct amount of sales tax for every transaction.

Pro Tip: Use a sales tax automation tool like Avalara or TaxJar. These tools are getting even smarter with machine learning, which can help you predict future obligations based on sales patterns, potentially saving you from costly surprises.

2. Crypto Tax Considerations – Know Before You HODL

When I attended the MIT Sloan Blockchain Technologies program, it became clear that cryptocurrency isn't a passing fad. It's a fundamental shift, much like the dawn of the internet. The IRS doesn't treat crypto as currency; it considers it property. This means that every transaction has tax implications, whether you're holding, selling, or accepting crypto as payment.

The crypto landscape can be tricky for newcomers and established businesses alike. But here's a simple rule: **If the world is getting more**

digital, the next "internet" is here, and cryptocurrency is part of it. Like it or not, crypto is here to stay, so if your business is involved, now is the time to stay compliant.

Key Points:

- **Accepting Crypto Payments**: You must report the fair market value (in USD) of the crypto payment on the day it's received.
- **Converting Crypto to Cash**: If you sell crypto and its value has increased since you received it, you owe capital gains tax.
- **Holding Crypto Long-Term**: If held over a year, you may qualify for lower long-term capital gains rates, unlike short-term holdings taxed as ordinary income.

It's also important to be aware of the tax implications of different crypto activities, such as mining, staking, and DeFi (decentralized finance) transactions. Each of these activities may have different reporting requirements and tax consequences. Consult with a tax professional specializing in cryptocurrency to ensure you're accurately reporting your crypto-related income and expenses.

Pro Tip: Consider using a crypto tracking tool like CoinTracking or ZenLedger to help with record-keeping, especially if you're processing high volumes of transactions. These tools offer reports that make IRS reporting far easier.

3. The Role of AI in Tax Compliance

AI has moved beyond mere automation—it's transforming how businesses track and manage their tax responsibilities. Machine learning algorithms can predict your tax obligations, track crypto market fluctuations, and anticipate when you might reach sales thresholds in specific states.

Real-World Example:

Imagine a business like an online boutique. It uses an AI-powered sales tracking tool that monitors sales by region and alerts the owner when it's nearing a state's tax threshold. This proactive approach allows the owner to make timely adjustments, file necessary paperwork, and avoid unexpected tax liabilities.

4. Case Study: How One E-commerce Brand Used AI to Stay Tax-Compliant

Sarah, the founder of an online boutique, relied on AI-driven insights to grow her business without the burden of surprise tax obligations. When Sarah expanded beyond her local state, her AI-enabled tracking tool monitored her sales volume in each state, helping her remain compliant with multi-state tax requirements. Instead of getting hit with unexpected bills, she stayed ahead with automated filings and real-time insights.

Sarah also used AI to analyze her sales data and identify which products were most popular in different states. This allowed her to optimize her inventory and marketing strategies, further increasing her profitability and ensuring she had the right products available in the states with the highest demand.

5. Case Study: How a Coffee Shop Made Crypto Payments Work

At BeanCoin Café, a small coffee shop that accepts Bitcoin, Ethereum, and even Dogecoin, the tax implications of crypto payments initially felt overwhelming. The café owner, Chris, didn't track the USD value of crypto payments on the day they were received, creating a tax headache. Chris pivoted, implementing Coinbase Commerce to manage transactions. Now, each crypto sale's dollar value is recorded on the spot, making tax season much smoother.

Chris also discovered that accepting crypto payments attracted a new segment of tech-savvy customers to his café. This not only boosted his sales but also enhanced his brand image as a forward-thinking business.

6. Practical Tips for Staying on Top of Taxes in E-commerce and Crypto

Navigating taxes can be complex, but some basic steps can keep you on track:

- **Automate Sales Tax**: Use tools like Avalara or TaxJar for multi-state sales tax calculations and filings.
- **Track Crypto Transactions in Real-Time**: Crypto transactions are increasingly being scrutinized, so keep real-time records using tools like CoinTracking.
- **Use AI for Forecasting**: AI-driven forecasting tools can help anticipate tax obligations, making compliance far simpler and less manual.
- **Consult a Professional**: The landscape is ever-changing. Working with experts like The Nealson Group can make all the difference in staying compliant.

If your e-commerce business or crypto activities extend beyond the United States, it's essential to understand the international tax implications. Different countries have varying tax laws and regulations, and navigating these complexities can be challenging. Consult with a tax advisor specializing in international taxation to ensure you're meeting your global tax obligations.

Wrap-Up: Staying Ahead in a Digital World

Taxes and regulations are challenging, especially in the fast-paced digital era. As a business owner, staying compliant means staying aware. You're not only keeping up with changes in e-commerce and crypto but also positioning yourself for long-term success. The right tools, automation, and professional guidance make all the difference.

And remember, you don't have to do it alone. The Nealson Group can help you navigate these waters, keeping you focused on what you do best: growing your business.

Bonus Chapter 3: Navigating the World of AI – Tools, Trends, and Risks

"The future belongs to those who prepare for it today." – Malcolm X

This chapter provides you with practical advice on AI adoption, real-world examples, and ethical considerations—ensuring they're ready to embrace new technology without losing sight of what matters most: people. Enjoy.

Introduction: AI Isn't Sci-Fi Anymore—It's Here to Help Your Business

Imagine a world where your business operates with the efficiency of a well-oiled machine, your marketing efforts hit the bullseye every time, and your customers feel like you're reading their minds. This isn't science fiction; it's the power of AI in action. Artificial intelligence has moved beyond the realm of futuristic fantasies and is now a tangible tool that can revolutionize businesses of all sizes.

Artificial Intelligence (AI) has shifted from sci-fi dreams to daily reality, transforming how businesses plan, interact, and make decisions. Imagine streamlining operations, automating marketing, or predicting customer needs effortlessly—it's possible with AI, even for small businesses. This chapter will explore practical ways to incorporate AI into your business and offer a roadmap to balance its benefits with ethical considerations, so you can stay competitive without losing the human touch.

1. AI Tools for Business Planning, Marketing, and Customer Service

AI can feel like having a virtual team, ready to boost productivity and enhance customer experiences. Let's see how AI fits into your daily operations:

Business Planning:

AI-powered tools like ChatGPT help small business owners make sense of data quickly, offering answers to complex questions without hours spent in spreadsheets. Ask, *"What should our sales goals be for next quarter based on this year's growth?"* and get an instant, data-backed forecast.

Beyond ChatGPT, tools like **PlanGuru** and **Adaptive Insights** offer AI-powered forecasting and budgeting capabilities that can help you make data-driven decisions about resource allocation, pricing strategies, and growth initiatives.

Marketing Automation:
AI personalizes marketing by predicting customer behavior and optimizing campaigns. For example, HubSpot's AI can identify leads most likely to convert, suggest content ideas, and optimize email campaigns—saving you time while increasing conversions.

AI can also personalize website content and product recommendations in real-time, ensuring that each customer sees the most relevant information. Platforms like **Personyze** and **OptiMonk** specialize in AI-driven website personalization.

Customer Service:
Chatbots like Intercom and Drift provide 24/7 service, handling inquiries and even upselling based on browsing history. And when human support is needed, bots can smoothly hand over the conversation. The trick is to choose bots that integrate with your CRM, allowing for seamless tracking of customer interactions.

AI can also analyze customer sentiment in real-time, allowing you to identify and address potential issues before they escalate. Tools like **MonkeyLearn** and **Repustate** can analyze customer feedback from various channels, providing valuable insights into customer satisfaction and areas for improvement.

"People don't buy what you do; they buy why you do it." – Simon Sinek

This quote highlights a key point—AI should support your mission, not overshadow it. Use it to enhance customer experience and efficiency but keep the heart of your business personal.

2. Real-World Examples of AI in Action

Here are examples of how real businesses are embracing AI to transform their operations:

- **Example 1: Automating Personalized Marketing in a Retail Store**

  Imagine a retail brand using AI-powered software to analyze customer purchasing patterns and predict the best times to send marketing emails. A small clothing boutique implemented AI-driven recommendations; tailoring promotions based on each customer's browsing history. The result? A 20% increase in engagement and a 15% boost in sales during targeted campaigns.

- **Example 2: Optimizing Supply Chain with Predictive AI**

  A mid-sized restaurant chain used AI to predict demand based on past sales data and seasonal trends, allowing it to optimize its inventory orders. With AI's help, the restaurant cut down on waste by 30% and saved significant costs, all while maintaining the quality and freshness customers expect.

- **Example 3: AI-Powered Fraud Detection in a FinTech Startup**

  In the world of finance, fraud is a constant threat. A FinTech startup implemented AI algorithms trained to detect unusual patterns in transaction data. The AI flagged potentially fraudulent activity in real time, saving the company thousands of dollars in losses and ensuring customer trust.

- **Example 4: Streamlining Hiring Processes with AI**

  A small tech company used an AI-driven recruitment tool to screen applications, quickly identifying qualified candidates based on criteria like skillsets and work history. This not only saved time but helped remove potential human biases in the hiring process, leading to a more diverse and inclusive team.

- **Example 5: AI-Powered Healthcare Diagnostics:**

  A medical clinic implemented an AI-powered diagnostic tool that analyzes patient data and medical images to assist doctors in identifying potential health issues with greater accuracy and speed.

  - **Example 6: AI-Driven Agricultural Optimization:**

  A farming operation used AI to analyze soil conditions, weather patterns, and crop health, optimizing irrigation and fertilization schedules to increase yields and reduce resource consumption.

  - **Example 7: AI-Enabled Educational Personalization:**

  An online education platform used AI to personalize learning paths for students, recommending relevant courses and providing customized feedback based on their individual progress and learning styles.

3. Risks and Ethical Considerations When Implementing AI

As powerful as AI is, it comes with its own set of risks. Addressing these challenges helps your business thrive responsibly:

Data Privacy:
AI relies on data to learn and adapt, but handling sensitive information requires caution. Data breaches are costly and damage customer trust. Implementing strong security measures and clearly communicating your data policies to customers is critical.

To mitigate data privacy risks, consider implementing techniques like data anonymization and differential privacy, which allow you to analyze data without compromising individual identities.

Bias in Algorithms:
AI tools reflect the data they're trained on, meaning that biases in the

data can lead to unintended consequences. An example of this occurred with early facial recognition systems that had higher error rates for people with darker skin tones. As a result, businesses should regularly evaluate AI outputs for bias, especially when algorithms influence critical areas like hiring or customer segmentation.

It's crucial to ensure that the data used to train AI algorithms is diverse and representative of the populations your business serves. Regularly audit your AI systems for bias and make necessary adjustments to ensure fairness and equity.

Maintaining the Human Touch:
Efficiency is great, but customers still value human interaction. While a chatbot can answer questions in seconds, it can't always replicate the reassurance of a real conversation. A simple, "Can I help you with anything else?" from a person can significantly boost customer loyalty.

Consider using AI to augment human capabilities rather than replacing them entirely. For example, AI can provide customer service representatives with real-time insights and recommendations, empowering them to provide more personalized and efficient support.

Pro Tip: Use AI to automate repetitive tasks and let your employees focus on meaningful interactions. Striking this balance keeps your brand human centered.

4. Case Study: How a Small Business Used AI-Powered Chatbots to Reduce Costs and Improve Satisfaction

Let's meet Lisa, the owner of an online bookstore. Managing customer inquiries, especially during busy seasons, became a challenge. Customers wanted to know if certain books were in stock, when orders would arrive, and how to apply discount codes.

Lisa implemented a Drift chatbot to handle frequent questions. Here's how AI transformed her business:

- **Labor Savings**: The chatbot handled 80% of inquiries, reducing the need for additional customer support staff.

- **Improved Customer Experience**: The bot offered instant answers, decreasing wait times and boosting satisfaction.
- **Increased Sales**: By suggesting related books based on customers' browsing, the bot increased sales by 15%.

Lisa also ensured that the chatbot's responses were aligned with her brand's voice and values. She personalized the chatbot's interactions, making it feel like a friendly and helpful assistant rather than a cold and impersonal machine. This attention to detail further enhanced the customer experience and strengthened customer loyalty.

The takeaway? Lisa's bookstore grew without chaos, thanks to AI that enhanced, rather than replaced, customer service.

5. Practical Tips for Integrating AI Without Losing the Human Touch

AI can be transformative, but thoughtful integration is key. Here's how to keep it smart and simple:

1. **Start Small**: Pilot an AI tool for a specific function—like using chatbots for customer service—before expanding its role in your business.
2. **Choose Tools That Fit**: Not every business needs advanced AI software. Sometimes, simple automation tools like Zapier can streamline workflows.
3. **Keep Your Team Informed**: AI performs best when teams understand its purpose and functionality. Offer training to ensure everyone is comfortable.
4. **Regularly Evaluate AI**: Monitor performance metrics— whether for marketing or customer service—and adjust based on results.
5. **Embrace the Human Touch**: Use AI to simplify processes so that employees can focus on quality interactions with customers.

6. Future of AI

The field of AI is constantly evolving, with new advancements emerging rapidly. Stay informed about the latest trends and innovations, such as generative AI, which can create new content and automate creative tasks, and edge computing, which brings AI processing closer to the data source, enabling faster and more efficient applications. By staying ahead of the curve, you can position your business to leverage the full potential of AI in the years to come.

Wrap-Up: Embrace AI, But Stay Human

The potential of AI is enormous, offering small businesses innovative ways to streamline, predict, and connect with customers. However, it's essential to remember that behind every transaction is a person. AI can take on the routine, but it's the human moments that build lasting loyalty.

Takeaway Tips:

- Use AI tools like ChatGPT to save time and make smarter decisions.
- Automate repetitive tasks to improve efficiency.
- Be aware of risks, like data privacy and algorithmic bias.
- Keep the human touch alive to build customer trust and loyalty.

And remember, if AI seems overwhelming, you're not alone. The Nealson Group is here to guide you, ensuring that AI integration fits seamlessly into your business while keeping customer relationships at the heart of what you do.

Bonus Chapter 4: Business Formation – When to Go from LLC to S Corp (and Beyond)

"Your business structure is the foundation upon which your empire will be built." –
Unknown

*This chapter provides practical tax advice, an easy-to-understand case study, and
leaves you empowered to make informed decisions about your business structure.
Thank you for sticking with me on this journey to a stronger financial foundation.*

Introduction: Your Business Structure Isn't Just Paperwork—It's a Financial Strategy

Choosing the right business structure isn't just a formality. It impacts
everything: the taxes you pay, the protection of your personal assets,
and your administrative responsibilities. Think of it like picking the
right workout plan: you need one that aligns with your lifestyle and
business goals. In this chapter, we'll outline common business
structures and walk you through when it might be time to move from
an LLC to an S Corp. Plus, we'll share real-world examples and a
decision-making checklist.

1. The Basics of Business Structures – Finding the Right Fit for Your Business

Let's start by breaking down the common business structures and their
pros and cons:

Sole Proprietorship
This is the simplest form, ideal for freelancers or small businesses just
starting out.

This structure is often chosen by solopreneurs, consultants, and
freelancers who operate independently and have minimal liability
concerns.

- *Pros*: Easy setup, minimal paperwork, and direct reporting of income on your personal tax return.
- *Cons*: Personal liability for all business debts, plus self-employment tax on all income.

LLC (Limited Liability Company)

An LLC protects personal assets and offers some tax flexibility, but profits are still subject to self-employment tax.

LLCs are popular among small businesses and startups because they offer liability protection and flexible taxation options. Members of an LLC can choose to be taxed as a sole proprietorship, partnership, or S corporation.

- *Pros*: Limited liability with less formality and flexibility in taxation.
- *Cons*: Self-employment tax can eat into profits if you don't elect S Corp status.

S Corporation (S Corp)

An S Corp isn't a separate entity but a tax election, offering tax savings if your business is profitable.

S corporations are often favored by growing businesses with significant profits because they can offer substantial tax savings compared to other structures. However, they require more stringent record-keeping and compliance procedures.

- *Pros*: Avoids self-employment tax on a portion of profits by dividing income into salary and distributions.
- *Cons*: More administrative work, including payroll requirements and formal record-keeping.

"Good fortune is what happens when opportunity meets with planning." – Thomas Edison

This quote captures the essence of business structure decisions. Choosing the right structure is about planning ahead and optimizing for growth.

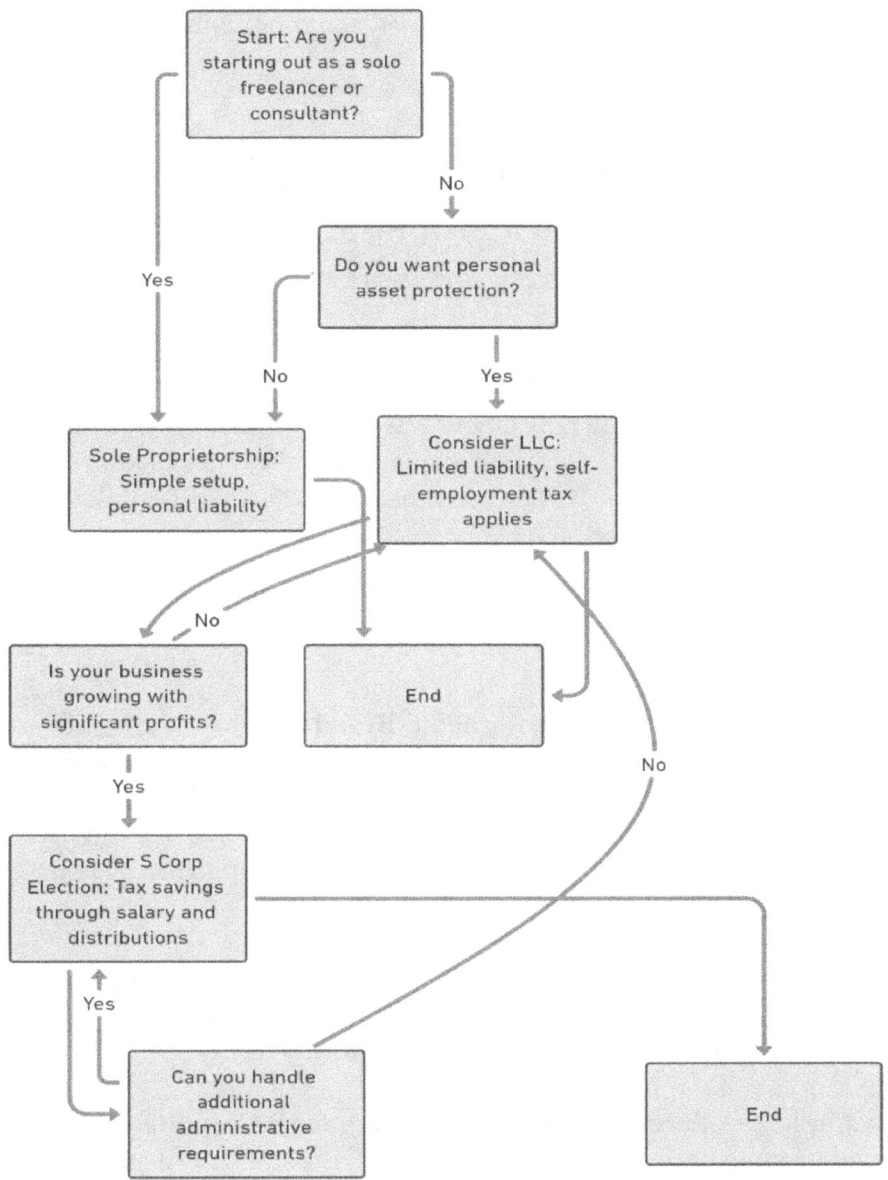

2. When to Switch to an S Corp – Unlocking Tax Savings

Knowing when to switch from an LLC to an S Corp often depends on profits. If your business consistently nets more than $50,000–$80,000 annually, the S Corp structure can help reduce your tax liability.

Key Example:

- **Paying Yourself:** As an LLC, you pay self-employment tax on all earnings. But with an S Corp, you can divide your income between a "reasonable" salary (subject to payroll taxes) and distributions (not subject to self-employment tax).

Real-World Example

- *Example:* Casey, a consultant, was making $120,000 annually through an LLC. After switching to an S Corp and setting a salary of $60,000, Casey saved nearly $9,000 in self-employment taxes.

3. Real-World Examples of Businesses Switching to S Corps for Tax Savings

Example 1: A Growing E-commerce Brand

Emma runs an online home goods store that started small but quickly scaled. When her profits exceeded $100,000, her CPA advised switching to an S Corp. By structuring her income as $60,000 in salary and $40,000 in distributions, she reduced her self-employment tax significantly.

Emma also appreciated the increased credibility that came with being an S corporation. It gave her business a more professional image and made it easier to secure funding from investors.

Example 2: A Service-Based LLC Opting for S Corp Status

A landscaping business in Texas, structured as an LLC, had annual profits of $85,000. The owners found themselves facing high self-employment taxes. By converting to an S Corp, they saved over $6,500 on taxes in their first year. They used payroll software to streamline compliance, making the switch worthwhile without extra administrative burden.

The owners also found that the S corporation structure allowed them to offer employee benefits more easily, which helped them attract and retain skilled workers.

Example 3: A Solo Law Firm in Florida
Melissa, a solo attorney, initially registered her firm as an LLC. With profits exceeding $90,000, she switched to an S Corp. Dividing her income into a reasonable salary and distributions allowed her to reduce her tax burden significantly, while also adding retirement contributions through an S Corp setup.

Melissa also discovered that the S corporation structure provided her with greater flexibility in planning for retirement, allowing her to contribute pre-tax income to a retirement account.

Example 4: A Boutique Marketing Agency in California
Jason and his team built a marketing agency with steady profits and were structured as an LLC. By switching to an S Corp, Jason could take a salary and additional distributions. This strategy saved him thousands and allowed him to reinvest tax-efficiently into the business, helping it grow faster without overextending.

Jason and his team also found that the S corporation structure made it easier to attract and retain talented employees by offering them equity in the company

"Don't wait. The time will never be just right." – Napoleon Hill

This quote reminds business owners not to delay important structural changes. If profits are increasing, now is the time to evaluate your structure and potentially move to an S Corp.

4. Case Study: How a Freelancer Saved Thousands by Switching to an S Corp

Meet Jamie, a graphic designer who began as a single-member LLC. For a while, Jamie's income held steady at $40,000 annually. But as her business grew and profits hit $100,000, her tax burden grew significantly.

Here's how switching to an S Corp helped Jamie:

- *Tax Savings*: Jamie saved over $7,500 in self-employment taxes her first year by splitting her income between a salary and distributions.
- *Easy Administration*: By using payroll software, she found the extra work manageable and well worth the savings.

Jamie discovered that the S corporation structure allowed her to contribute to a retirement plan, something she couldn't do as easily as an LLC. This provided her with additional tax benefits and helped her plan for her long-term financial security.

5. Decision-Making Checklist – Should You Switch to an S Corp?

Switching isn't right for every business. Here's a checklist to help determine if it's the right move for you:

- Is your business consistently making over $50,000 in net profit?
- Are you comfortable with payroll and additional record-keeping?
- Are you looking to reinvest profits tax-efficiently?
- Do you have fewer than 100 shareholders (a requirement for S Corps)?
- Are you okay with the added paperwork?

While this chapter focused on LLCs and S corporations, there are other business structures to consider, such as partnerships, C corporations, and B corporations. Each structure has its own unique characteristics, advantages, and disadvantages. It's essential to research and understand all your options before making a decision. A business attorney or tax advisor can provide guidance on which structure is most suitable for your specific needs and goals.

"Success usually comes to those who are too busy to be looking for it." – Henry David Thoreau

This quote underscores the value of seeking expert advice. A trusted advisor like The Nealson Group can save you time and money by helping you choose the right business structure without getting bogged down in administrative details.

6. How the Nealson Group Can Help

Navigating business structures can be daunting. The Nealson Group specializes in helping small business owners evaluate their options, stay compliant, and make the best choices for long-term success.

Here's how we support you:

- **Customized Advice**: We assess your current structure and guide you through the best options.
- **Smooth Transition**: We help with S Corp elections and set up payroll so you're always compliant.
- **Ongoing Support**: Our team offers tax planning and accounting services to keep your business focused on growth.

Wrap-Up: Choose the Structure That Works for You

Your business structure isn't just paperwork—it's a strategic choice with real financial consequences. Whether you stay with an LLC, move to an S Corp, or explore other options, the key is finding a structure that aligns with your goals.

"The secret of getting ahead is getting started." – Mark Twain

If you're unsure where to start, reach out to The Nealson Group. We're here to guide you, making the process easier so you can focus on what matters most: growing your business.

Remember, your business structure is not set in stone. As your business grows and evolves, you may need to re-evaluate your structure and consider making changes to optimize your tax strategy and legal protections. Stay informed, seek expert advice, and make proactive decisions that support your long-term vision.

ABOUT THE AUTHOR

Chris is a CPA and has an MBA in Finance, but his journey wasn't exactly a straight line. At 26, he bought a blues bar, where "financial literacy" meant trashing financial reports after pretending to read them. (Hey, we've all been there, right?)

He's since become a CPA, working in tax and audit for a top national firm and serving as CFO for multi-million dollar companies. But don't worry, he's not your typical boring accountant. With a background in customer service, from nightclubs to the Ritz-Carlton, he knows how to explain complex financial stuff in a way that actually makes sense.

As a serial entrepreneur himself, Chris gets the challenges of business ownership. Now, he's on a mission to help you take control of your finances, one simple conversation at a time.

Glossary of Terms

Assets: Everything your business owns that has value. Think of it as your "business bling" - the cash, equipment, and even the money owed to you.

Balance Sheet: A snapshot of what you own (assets) versus what you owe (liabilities). It's like a financial selfie, showing your business's net worth at a specific moment.

Break-Even Point: The sales level where your revenue covers all your costs. It's like that sigh of relief when you finally start making money instead of just throwing it around.

Budget: A plan for how you'll spend your money. Think of it as a diet for your business finances - it helps you avoid overspending and keeps you financially trim.

Burn Rate: How quickly a startup uses its cash reserves. It's like measuring how fast you're going through a pile of cash. Hopefully not as fast as a bonfire at a music festival.

Cash Flow: The movement of cash in and out of your business. It's the lifeblood of your business - you need it to pay the bills, buy inventory, and keep the lights on.

Cash Flow Forecast: Predicting your future cash flow situation. It's like checking the financial weather forecast - it helps you prepare for potential storms or sunny days ahead.

COGS (Cost of Goods Sold): The direct costs of producing the goods you sell. It's what you pay for ingredients if you're a bakery or the cost of materials if you're a manufacturer.

Cryptocurrency: Digital currencies like Bitcoin and Ethereum. It's the cool, futuristic way to get paid, but remember, the value can fluctuate wildly - like a rollercoaster ride for your finances.

Customer Acquisition Cost (CAC): How much it costs to get a new customer. It's the price you pay for those "Welcome aboard!" emails.

Customer Lifetime Value (CLTV): The predicted total revenue from a single customer throughout their relationship with your business. It's like calculating how much "bang for your buck" you get from each customer.

Days Sales Outstanding (DSO): How long it takes customers to pay you. If it takes longer than a new Taylor Swift album to drop, you need to send some friendly reminders (or maybe a carrier pigeon).

Disengaged Employees: Employees who are not emotionally connected to their work or company. They're like that friend who's always "meh" about everything - not very productive or profitable.

Financial Clarity: Understanding your business's financial health. It's like wiping the fog off your windshield so you can see where you're going (and avoid that financial ditch).

Financial Planning: Setting financial goals and creating a roadmap to achieve them. It's like planning a road trip for your business - you need a destination and a route to get there.

Financial Strategy: Aligning your long-term vision with your financial reality. It's like having a GPS for your business - it helps you stay on track and reach your destination.

Forecasting: Predicting future financial performance. It's like having a crystal ball for your business - it helps you anticipate trends and make better decisions.

Free Shipping: A popular e-commerce tactic that can be costly if not managed strategically. It's like giving away free candy - it might attract customers, but it can also eat into your profits.

Gross Profit Margin: The percentage of revenue left after covering the direct costs of goods sold. It's how much money you make from selling your product before all those other expenses come knocking.

HOA (Homeowners Association): A well-meaning organization that strives to create a harmonious community where everyone's lawn is perfectly manicured, no basketball hoops dare grace a driveway, and the only acceptable color for your front door is "Beige Majesty."

Inventory Management: Keeping track of your products and ensuring you have the right amount in stock. It's like walking a tightrope - you don't want too much or too little.

KPIs (Key Performance Indicators): Metrics that measure your business's performance. They're like your business's report card - they tell you how you're doing in different areas.

Liabilities: Everything your business owes to others. Think of it as your "business debt" - loans, credit card balances, and those "oops, I forgot to pay that" moments.

Net Profit Margin: The percentage of revenue left after covering all expenses. It's the real MVP - the money you get to keep after everyone else has taken their cut.

Profit: The money you make after deducting expenses from revenue. It's the reason you're in business - to make money, not just spend it.

Profit per Employee: A measure of how much profit your business generates for each employee. It's like a productivity scorecard for your team - the higher the score, the better.

Profitless Growth: Increasing revenue without increasing profit. It's like running on a treadmill - you're working hard, but not really getting anywhere.

Revenue: The total income your business generates from sales. It's the top line of your income statement - the big, flashy number that everyone likes to talk about.

SMART Goals: Goals that are Specific, Measurable, Achievable, Relevant, and Time-bound. It's the goal-setting framework that helps you actually achieve your goals instead of just dreaming about them.

Upselling: Offering customers additional products or services to increase their order value. It's like that "Would you like fries with that?" moment - a subtle way to boost sales.